# CREATE
# LIFETIME
# LOYAL
# CUSTOMERS

# CREATE LIFETIME LOYAL CUSTOMERS

*7 Success Principles to Attract More Customers in
ANY Business Even in the Toughest Economies*

C A R R I E   A N N E   Y U

PARTRIDGE

**To order additional copies of this book, contact**
Toll Free 800 101 2657 (Singapore)
Toll Free 1 800 81 7340 (Malaysia)
orders.singapore@partridgepublishing.com

www.partridgepublishing.com/singapore

# Table of Contents

# DEDICATION

Thanks my Mom & Dad
for their unconditional love and lifetime support

# Acknowledgments

A big thanks to my sister, Cathy Yu, for all our fantastic years together. Christine Yung, Jenlen Ng, Steve Bernstein, Simon McConnell, Dr Andrew Stotz and Tai Lopez deserve special mention for their inspiration, support and advice. A special thanks to my mentor Joel Bauer for everything his suggestions have contributed to this book.

# Introduction

Suppose there was one thing – just one – that you could change about yourself, your business or the trade or profession you find yourself in. What would it be? What would you pick out as the single most important change to make?

Something that made it easier to attract the kind of customers you most want? Something mean that your customers, and the people you would like to become your customers, would see you as highly professional – the go-to person in your line of business?

Perhaps everything is going swimmingly for you right now, but even so you'd like to raise your performance level to become better at objection handling and up your closure rate, get more repeat business, improve your effectiveness and be more persuasive?

If you're going to be a winner, your customers have to feel that there is only one solution for them, and that solution is your business. Do you do everything you can to make that happen? Do you get them to a place where they believe no one but you really understand their problem; what they need is so special and so unique, that only one person really understands it, and this person is you?

And then there are referrals. Just for a moment, get into your head a picture of your best customers. Decide what it is about them that makes them the best. Now imagine being in touch with so many new contacts who match those best customers in every regard that you're not sure you can handle them all. Now; what is it that you could change about you, your business or the way you conduct it that would put you in that position? You'd be more productive in business. You'd be better in business. And you'd be happier. So what does the change need to be?

All these questions will be covered in this book, but that's not all you'll get; we'll also be talking about the things that make the critical difference between *success* and *being just-another-business*. The ideas we are going to explore, the methods and techniques that you can use immediately, are all proven. They'll help you get more sales, improve business performance, solve the biggest challenges you face, earn more money, improve your work/life balance, and enjoy yourself more while you're at it.

Who could possibly pass up an opportunity like that?

# Become More Effective

The world is changing. Nothing new there; the world has always changed. What's different is the sheer speed of change – in a single lifetime now, a whole industry can come into being, thrive and die. That's always happened, but in the old days, it might take three, four, or five generations. Now, it can be as short as ten years. Technology becomes more complex, competition becomes sharper, you have less time to get your product to market, cover your costs and make money, and the people you are looking to sell it to are, by and large, better educated. It's a challenge. Challenges are there to be met. This book tells you how.

Customers have more choice, and not only in the services and products they decide to buy, but in the person or business they decide to buy it from. The winners in this business battle will be those who take time to understand and meet their customers' needs and to become more professional in the way they do it.

Even if you're doing okay, you still need to be constantly improving. That's the way the world is today. The service you provide, the effectiveness of your products, the way you solve problems when they arise, your sales and marketing techniques – all of them need constant updating. Here's something you've almost certainly heard from others:

**"People don't care how much you know,
until they know how much you care."**

So make a point of helping your customers solve their problems in a way they find professional, and cost-effective.

# Be Open To New Ideas

The purpose of this book is to show you how to be the best you can be. I don't claim the book has the answer to every single problem your business will ever face. You won't find that anywhere. What this book does offer is concepts, ideas and techniques that have worked for people like you in situations like yours.

That in itself is not enough, but it's all I can do – the rest has to come from you. When you have absorbed the ideas and information in this book, you then have to decide which is right for you and your business, and how to employ them to best effect.

Something else this book does not claim to do is to make you a marketing ninja. The object is to give you tools that are working in successful people's businesses today. We'll be looking at ways of increasing sales, improving marketing and customer service, and building your business that have already earned serious money for others.

Some of the ideas you come across in this book will be easy to put into practice right away. Others may take a little longer. And there may be some that just aren't applicable to your business. That's cool; a world in which every single one of the same things worked every single time for every single business would be very boring. But you will, without question, be able to benefit from implementing a significant number. And the difference they make to your business will mean that your time studying this book has been well spent.


# How We Receive, Process and Store Information

Of course, it's good to get new ideas, and this book will give you plenty – but getting new ideas is only part of the process. A new idea that stays in your head does you no good at all. You have to put it into practice. Here are some interesting figures:

WE REMEMBER:

- 86% of what we see, hear and DO!
- 56% of what we see and hear
- 37% of what we see

- 22% of what we hear
- 10% of what we read

So, if you want these new ideas to bear fruit in the form of a more successful business, reading about them is not enough. You have to put them into practice, and you have to do it before you have forgotten them. Your customers are waiting for you to provide something in which they will see value. Don't let them down

Jeffrey Pfeffer and Robert Sutton wrote a book, *The Knowing-Doing Gap* on this very subject. According to them, each year sees:

- $60 billion spent on training
- 1,700 new business books published
- $43 billion paid to consultants
- 80,000 new MBAs.

And still, the authors say, most businesses carry on in the same way as they always have. Knowing is not enough. If you don't do something with what you know, you might as well not have picked this book up.

This book will not be full of airy-fairy ideas, blue sky thinking or speculative concepts. I'm not offering you unproven theories. What you get here will be the ideas and methods that are being put into practice with great success all over the world. Day in, and day out. Take the time to understand what I'm saying, and to make whatever adjustments you need to make so that they are applicable to your business, and they'll work for you as they work for others.

## Learning and Retention; the Five Steps

Knowledge comprises two components (acquiring new information, and remembering it) and consists of five steps:

**Inspiration**. You begin with a new idea or a new concept. It doesn't matter whether it's a word you read or heard, a picture you saw, something you experienced or whether it came to you in some totally different way – it's in your mind. Don't stop there.

Here's something for you to try. Sit somewhere comfortable. Make sure your feet are resting flat on the floor, and your hands are in your lap and comfortable. Close your eyes. Take a deep breath. Let the breath out slowly. Relax. Do it again – deep breath in, let it out slowly, relax.

Now, imagine that on the table in front of you (keep your eyes closed) is a tangerine. Without opening your eyes, "see" the tangerine. Its shape. That characteristic tangerine color – so characteristic, in fact, that the tangerine has given its name to that color on decorator charts. See the texture and the size.

Still without opening your eyes, imagine you are reaching out a hand. You're picking up the tangerine. You're bringing it close. You're handling it – squeezing it. Feel how firm it is? How the texture is? The shape – round, but a little flat on top and bottom, like a pumpkin?

Now smell it. Then – and remember, this is still in your mind, you're not actually doing it – use your thumb to peel it. Sniff again – the smell should be stronger now. Imagine taking off a segment and biting into it.

Now – what do you feel? Ready to eat a tangerine? Are those feelings both physical and in your mind?

What was this exercise about? You didn't have a tangerine, it was purely imaginary, so this was an exercise of the mind. What you almost certainly found was that those mental images in your mind triggered physical responses in your body. What you have just shown yourself is that inspiration is a first step in acquiring knowledge.

**Iteration.** An iterative process is one that is repeated again and again. Iteration means repetition. It's where the word "reiteration" comes from. Research says something you've heard, read or seen only once has a 66% chance of being forgotten in the next 24 hours. Those odds are transformed to a 90% likelihood that you will remember it when the same inspiration process is reiterated regularly for eight days.

What we can take from that is, if you read this book and then read it again – ideally in a slightly different way, for example, jotting ideas down in a notebook or underlining sections of text – you will retain much more of the information that if you read it only once.

**Application**. In this context, by "application" we mean "doing." There is a facility that some call "mind-muscle memory;" it is actually the development of neuron pathways in the brain. One of the things it means is that physically experiencing an action makes it twice as easy to remember and recall to mind as something you have heard, and heard only once.

**Internalization.** An idea that sits in your head and is not translated into action (Application) is generally wasted. Internalization means making an idea part of you, so that it informs and directs the way you behave. Ideally, internalization is accompanied by customizing, so that you take the ideas you find in this book, adapt them to become a perfect fit with your business and situation, and then make them part of the overall you. It's much harder to internalize something that you have not first customized.

**Reinforcement.** It's easy to think that, by the time we have an idea internalized, it's ours and we are ready to run with it. That's only partly true. To really get the most from an idea, you have to keep returning to it, strengthening it and repeating it. That is the way that ideas become totally effective and help us become the kind of business that people want to deal with.

This book contain many great ideas. Don't read them in a vacuum – but all times, have in mind your own business and your own activities, so that you can identify those that will be of help to you. Some of the ideas may be completely new to you; some you may have heard and forgotten; and it's quite possible that others will trigger memories or previous inspirations that you meant to do something about, but didn't. As you discover each idea, please don't forget to apply the five learning and retention steps (the steps to "Knowledge") that we just worked through.

## It's Only When You Act That Things Happen

One of my clients when I have my business consultant hat on told me about the time, several years ago, when he was trained as a salesman by IBM. He thought some of the sales methods he and the other trainees were taught were great, some he had doubts about, and he said that one or two appeared to him to be foolish – he thought, "No one is ever going to fall for that. I can't see myself ever using it outside sales school."

One day, a couple of years after they'd made him an IBM quota salesman, he was calling on a new prospect. It wasn't going well. In fact, it was clear that my client was never going to make a sale to this man. This was exactly the sort of situation in which IBM had suggested one of their procedures would be useful – one of those that he had rejected as impossible to put into practice. Knowing he wasn't going to get anything out of this call, he thought, "Well, why not? What have you got to lose?" He went ahead and delivered the message IBM had suggested.

'The prospect, for the first time during that meeting, looked thoughtful. He scratched his chin. Then he looked at me – the first open, sincere and engaged look he had given me – and he said, "Yes. I can see that makes sense. Well, how do we put this into action?"'

The lesson my client learned that day, and the lesson I now invite you to learn, is to keep an open mind. Don't judge an idea before you've tried it, and don't assume that, because you think it might not work on you, it won't work on anyone else. There's only one way to find out how good an idea is, and that is to put it into practice.

Here are some things I suggest you might want to think about:

- An idea is not new to you, but you've never used it. Ask yourself: "Why not?"
- You are using an idea. Ask yourself: "How well am I using it? What can I do to improve my use of it, and make it work better both the business and for me?"
- For every idea for which you have gone through the five learning steps previously listed, as yourself: "What would happen if I used that? What would the results be?" Then, DO it, and see whether you were right – check the actual results against the ones you thought there would be.

What I'm trying to do in this book is to persuade you to turn theory into action. To take what you have learned and to DO it. Having a head stuffed full of knowledge is great, but it doesn't actually achieve anything on its own. What you have to do is put the things you have learned into action. Not just a test that, but to freshen up your business, keep it alive and keep it growing. Good ideas on their own do nothing. Good ideas put into practice bring you fun, a thriving business, and *PROFIT.*

Just don't forget to customize – be careful to adapt ideas to the circumstances of the business and the market that you are in.

# So What Is The Business You're In?

And, while you're adapting ideas to the business that you're in, please bear in mind one vital consideration which may just be the most important thing I say in this book:

How you **MARKET** your business is a lot more important than what **TYPE** of business it is.

Another way to put this is a well-known and very true salesman's slogan:

### *Sell the sizzle, not the steak*

A commonly used example is the insurance salesperson. Most insurance salespeople sell insurance, and that's an uphill battle and a tough sell, because most people don't want to buy insurance. But those same people don't want to buy insurance do want a number of other things:

- Security for themselves and their families
- The knowledge that their business will not disappear if the building is flooded or burned down
- A warm and comforting feeling that, should they be carried off to the great market in the sky before their time, leaving spouse and children behind, those loved ones will be looked after

And that's what good insurance salespeople sell – peace of mind. Warm, comforting feelings. What they *don't* sell, if they want a decent holiday at the end of the year, is the obligation to pay monthly premiums for the foreseeable future.

Now, we could find an insurance salesperson and ask, "Look. It's very obvious that people don't simply want to buy an insurance policy and an obligation to pay premiums. And we can see that they don't, because not enough insurance is sold. So, knowing that – why do you go on banging your head against the wall by trying to sell what people don't want to buy? What they do want to buy is peace of mind and warm, fuzzy feelings that they are doing the best they can for their families. So why on earth is that not what you are selling?"

Is it any wonder that, when people buy car insurance, they always look for the lowest rate? No, it isn't. But is the lowest rate the best marker for someone planning to buy car insurance? Once again: no, it isn't.

Don't be that salesperson trying to sell people what they don't want to buy. Sell the sizzle, not the steak – work out what it is that your product or service can give people that will make people feel good about themselves, because THAT is what will sell. In spades.

You're not in the insurance business? That doesn't matter. Whatever business you are in, begin by working out what it is that will make people really want to buy from you. Then tell the world: bang the drum, write it on the wall, have flyers printed, put it at the top of your website, and when a prospect asks what you do and why yours is the product or service they should buy, TELL THEM.

For a lot of businesses – and yours may be one of them – there isn't that much difference between the products they offer and the products a lot of other businesses offer. And, since overhead costs will likely be very similar, there may not be much difference between the price you need to charge and the price your nearest competitors need to charge. Some businesses may try loss-leaders for a while, but over the long term, the playing field is probably pretty level. What this means is:

**No business is likely to maintain a competitive advantage over the long term simply because of the goods or services it provides for the prices it charges**

So you're not going to build a long-term successful business that way. What you have to do is differentiate your business from the competition. Don't be a "Me Too," because there is neither fun nor future in that.

How do you avoid it? Examine your competitors closely. (And, unless you're selling something that can only be sold inside a fairly small geographic area (for example, you're a plumber or an electrician), look at what your competitors in other regions, other countries and on other continents are doing.

What should you be looking at? Their marketing, their advertising (no, those two things are not the same), the style in which they present themselves. And you know what you'll find? That they all look much the same as each other! Why? Because they really are in "Me Too" mode. Their attitude is: *This is what everyone else does, so we'd better do it this way, too.* And that's their weakness. That's the Achilles heel through which you will attack and defeat them.

Remember, if they always do what they've always done, they'll go on getting the same results they've always got. You want something better. And that means you want something different. What you have to do is find a different way of operating. And that will open the market and draw the customers to you.

I hope you're convinced, because it's time to move on to Chapter 1 and get you started!

*"The value of an idea lies in the using of it."*

Thomas Edison

# Principle 1

# What Makes Business Success

## The Tools You Need To Prosper

When I was starting out as a business consultant, I contacted some of the people I had have worked with and for. The reason was simple; I had my own ideas about what made some businesses more successful than others, but I wanted to hear what others thought, and especially to get the views of people with a record of high performance.

One of those people I contacted had a very interesting story to tell. He'd spent most of his working life in the UK and he had triumphed at a time and in a way that most people would have thought came somewhere between difficult and impossible. He'd launched a web-based service company in an industry that was already full (some might say there were too many players) and was dominated by huge companies with colossal amounts of money to spend. Money that meant that, if they needed to, they could see off a newcomer by reducing prices below cost level for as long as it took.

And yet, my contact and build a successful business and it wasn't him who'd had to pull out; it was one of those big companies that had threatened him. I asked (not unreasonably) what his secret was. He said it was simple. "In the last resort, it isn't about the product, the pricing, or the marketing. Sure, all those things are important, but what matters most is the level and quality of service you give to other people."

I asked how he had come by that insight.

"One of my earliest jobs was at the British furniture retailer, Cantor's. It had been going for a couple of generations by then, but a new member of the Cantor family had just taken over when his father died and he had a great idea. This was the 1960s and companies were just starting to use computers in a big way. Great big monsters they were, and expensive, and far less powerful than the chip in that smartphone you're holding, but they gave companies that used them an advantage over companies that didn't. And what the new young Managing Director understood was that, by monitoring stock levels and what sold in which store, he could greatly improve stock turnover. And he did.

"At that time, the typical British furniture store turned over its stock about once every 18 months. That's a disastrous amount of money to have tied up. At Cantor's, within two years, turnover had improved to 4 times a year. Much better return on investment; much lower borrowings; much more cash available for expansion, refurbishing stores, buying better stock – you name it."

"And that made the difference?" I asked.

He laughed. "No. That was the icing on the cake. What really made the difference was the effort he put into showing people how much he, his staff and the whole company cared about them. I'm not talking about sending out those flyers that everyone uses addressed to "Dear Valued Customer," because they fool no one. I'm talking about the change he made in the way that shop staff approached customers, talked to them, LISTENED to them, and made it clear that they were more interested in finding an answer to the customer's needs and wants than in selling a piece of furniture. And he added to that, because two days a week he was out there in the stores, talking to customers, listening to what they said, making notes, getting back to them. He cared about his customers and his customers knew he cared about them. He wanted to be of service to them. And he was. And they knew it.

"And THAT, my young friend, is what made his company so successful. And it's also what has made it possible for me to achieve what I have."

# The Mistake Failures Make

I learned a great deal from that story, and I have endeavored to pass it on to my clients and to help them find ways to show how THEY care. Those who have taken the lesson to heart – internalized it – show those same levels of success.

There will be times when you go to work and not a customer turns up. There will be times when someone makes a completely unreasonable comment or request. There will be times when you'd rather be at home, tucked up in bed with a hot drink and a good book. Those are the times when showing that you care (and, actually, you can only show that you care by actually CARING) feels like trying to push water uphill.

Keep pushing. Keep caring. Keep focusing on the customers' wants and needs and not on your own. Trust me: you will reap the benefit in time.

One other thing that fits here, but that I may very well want to say again later, is:

### *If you ignore a problem, it does not go away.*
### *It gets worse.*

Let's move on. You want to be a success in business. It's always possible, I suppose, that you will be lucky. You'll find yourself in the right place at the right time and everything will happen for you just as you would wish. Yes, that does happen. But don't count on it. In 999 cases out of 1,000, success comes after a great deal of hard work. How often have you heard it said of someone that, "S/he worked hard for 10 years to become an overnight sensation"?

Because that's what happens. You see someone suddenly become successful and it's so easy to think that it "just happened" for them. What you don't see is the work that went into it. Business success is like an iceberg; 90% of it is underwater and the casual sailor passing by only sees the 10% that shows.

If you really want to be a success (and, if you don't, why are you reading this book?) you need:

- An understanding of what makes for success
- A plan, carefully put together and just as carefully executed
- A definable set of personal characteristics.

This set, in fact:

# The Eight Characteristics Of Successful People

## 1. The ability to set goals

Be very clear about what you want from your business. Understand why you're there. Define your goals with clarity, and write them down just to make sure that you understand what they are. Return to that written statement regularly, so that you don't lose sight of where you are trying to get to.

One of the things you will get from doing that is the ability to stand back, stop for a moment working *in* your business and make time to work *on* it. You are not there for the benefit of your business. Your business is there for yours.

While you're doing this, spend some time analyzing where you started, where you are now, and where you want to be.

And *set goals*. Meaningful goals. If you don't do that, you run the risk of being sidetracked by every little issue and every little problem that crops up. Think of goals as signposts. They'll keep you pointed in the direction you want to go in.

How do you set goals? There's a well-tested set of rules; to have any real value, goals must be SMART:

- Specific
- Measurable
- Attainable
- Realistic
- Timebound

*Specific*, because you have to be clear about exactly what it is you are trying to achieve. Define the goal clearly and unambiguously. There must be no doubt about what it is, and none about whether or not you have reached it.

So, let's say one of your goals looks like this:

*Increase the number and value of sales per month*

Well, I'm sorry, but that is not specific enough. If you get one extra sale worth one extra dollar, will you have achieved your goal? If so, allow me to tell you that your goal was inadequate from the start. No, what that sort of goal should look like is:

*Get at least five more sales each month, and increase the*
*value of monthly sales by not less than $20,000*

THAT is a specific goal. Make sure all your goals are at least as specific as that one.

*Measurable* is tied into the example of a specific goal I've just given you. Make sure you have the tools in place to measure performance against your goals. Unless your bookkeeping system is totally inadequate, you will have a way of measuring with complete accuracy the value of sales you make each month, but do you have a way to count the customers? If not, install one.

And suppose one of your goals looks like this:

*Reduce to 3 months the time it takes to convert a*
*first time visitor to a paying customer*

That's specific, all right, but do you have a way to measure how long it takes to convert first-time visitors into customers? If you don't, you have no way of knowing whether you have met your target, and a target for which you can't tell whether or not you've achieved it is pointless – don't even bother setting it up.

Fortunately, the number of CRM (Customer Relationship Management) software packages now available means you can have this information at your fingertips – but that only helps if you actually look at the data from time to time. So the goal must not only be measurable; you must actually measure it.

*Attainable.* By "attainable," I don't just mean "realistic." I'll come to realistic in a moment. Requiring that a goal be attainable does not mean it should be easy. If it's easy, what's the point? Why are you setting yourself a goal you can easily achieve? The poet Robert Browning wrote these lines:

*Ah, but a man's reach should exceed his grasp, Or what's a heaven for?*

I'm with Browning. Make your goals things that you can achieve with hard work – sometimes, very hard work – but only if you stretch yourself to the limit.

*Realistic.* The key in the paragraph above is, "only if you stretch yourself to the limit" and the missing words are, "but not beyond." From time to time I see businessmen setting themselves targets that are estimable and praiseworthy in themselves – but completely useless, because they simply can't achieve them in the time they have set. And "useless" is inadequate as a description, because unrealistic goals are more than useless – they are damaging. If you have a goal and, however hard you work towards it, you never get there, it becomes discouraging.

*Timebound.* This really is a very important part of goal setting. It is very easy to set yourself a goal, but not have a time within which it must be accomplished. Really, that's not a goal at all, because you will never find yourself in a position of having to accept that you are missing it. Not setting a time limit is the same as setting a non-specific goal. It's vague. Now, some goals may be so big and involve such a long time scale that setting a time limit doesn't really involve pushing yourself. For example, suppose one of your goals is to move from the 1% of the total global market that you currently command to – say – 40%, and you believe that it will take you 10 years to do that. Well, simply setting a goal that says, *Grow market share from 1% to 40% in 10 years* is not satisfactory. It may be attainable. It may be realistic. It may be measurable. It is certainly, after a fashion, specific. But it isn't SMART because the time limit is so far in the future that no realistic monitoring can happen. The solution? Break it down. Set individual goals along the way. They may look like this:

*Grow market share from 1% to 3% in 1 year*
*Grow market share from 1% to 5% in 2 years*
*Grow market share from 1% to 8% in 3 years*

…and so on. Now you have SMART goals because they are all specific, measurable, attainable, realistic and timebound. If you get off track in achieving them, you will know early on that you are doing so, and you will be able to take steps to put matters right – to get back on schedule.

## 2. Having set goals, the ability to focus on them

As we have just seen, one of the characteristics that successful people have is the ability to set SMART goals. Another is the ability to focus. Amazing as this may seem, phenomenally successful business people do not have the amazing levels of foresight, perspicacity and financial whiz-kidery that you may contribute to them. When you meet them, as I have met some of them, the surprise is always that they are so…well…ordinary. There is, though, in every case, something that marks them out from the run of people, and that is: the ability to focus.

Set your goals. Focus on them, totally and constantly. And then you will become one of those same successful business people. Other people will be looking at you and thinking what amazing levels of foresight, perspicacity and financial whiz-kidery you must have.

You will be able to smile to yourself about it.

## 3. The willingness to pay the price of success

Everything has a price. For some of the things you most want in your drive to become a successful business person, the price is not expressed in money. It's about effort and dedication, and the amount you are prepared to put in.

An Australian, Eddie Jones, was put in charge of the England rugby union team after it had had a disastrous World Cup. In the year since then, and under the guidance of Eddie Jones, the England team has played eight matches against some of the strongest teams in the world and won all eight. They are now ranked second in the world, behind the New Zealand All Blacks. How did that happen? How did a team that had been the butt of jokes from Ireland to Australia more from that position to number two in the world in such a short time? It had nothing to do with luck, and everything to do with the work the players were prepared to put in and the price (in social life, in injuries, in time off) they were prepared to pay.

Eddie Jones himself made that very clear. He had at his disposal one of the best players in the world at either number 10 or number 15. The player's name is Danny Cipriani. Jones refuses to select him. Why? He was asked that question, and he answered it. Jones's preferred number 10 is Owen Farrell. His preferred number 15 is Mick Brown. They get the call, and Danny does not.

And the reason Jones prefers those two is that, in his words, "They want it enough to give up everything for it. They work so hard in training, they work so hard in the match. There's a price to pay to be in a side that will be a serious contender for the next World Cup. When Danny Cipriani shows the same willingness to give up everything for a place in this team, and puts physical fitness before everything else, I'll choose him for the squad. Until then, it isn't going to happen."

So, we are talking about sacrifice. Those successful people who have built businesses from nothing to world-class have been prepared to make the necessary sacrifices. The novelist William Golding knew all about this (and he won the Nobel Prize for Literature, so it's worth listening to what he has to say). In his novel, *Free Fall*, he put these words into the mouth of a headmaster speaking to a young man about to leave school and go into the world: "You can have anything you want, so long as you are prepared to make the necessary sacrifice."

And so can YOU.

But, if you are not prepared to pay the price and make the sacrifices, don't expect to take your place in the Business Hall of Fame. You won't make it.

What, in practice, will this mean? Well, it certainly won't mean risking having your leg broken on the rugby field. More likely, it will be things like going to see people where they are at times that are inconvenient to you. But here is a practical example from Nigeria.

A young man had started a road marking business in Lagos State. He bought his material from a very long established company based at that time in Texas though it is now in North Carolina (Ennis-Flint). Their African representative was based out of their EUMEA office in Europe. He was a man in his 60s who had refused to retire because he did not want to give up the pleasures of meeting new people and facing down new challenges. One day, when the young Nigerian (let's call him Matthew) had toiled for six or seven years to build a successful business, the Ennis-Flint representative (let's call him John) was in Lagos and went to lunch with Matthew to discuss what the next year held. Matthew said, "You know I followed your advice about my personal life?"

John had no recollection at all of advising Matthew on personal matters. "What advice was that?"

"Right at the beginning, when I was starting out. You said to me, 'Don't buy a Mercedes just yet. It will come in time, but for now, settle for something serviceable that doesn't cost much. Don't buy a house on the island. It will come in time, but for now, stick to a one-room apartment. Don't have a great big showy head office. You may have something like that later on, but for now, just put a Portakabin on your yard. If you ever think a customer is too important to come and see you there, meet them somewhere else. A cafe, maybe. But not at lunchtime and not at dinnertime. Go at a time when you can offer them a coffee and doughnut instead of a three course meal. And put all the money you save into the business. Buy not just more equipment, but better equipment – the best you can afford. Buy enough material that you never have to turn a job down because you don't have in stock what you would need to do it. Do all those things, and, I promise you, the Mercedes and the big house on the island will come. Eventually.' That's what you told me, and that's what I did."

"And has it worked?"

"Well, I've got the best equipment money can buy, and I don't owe a naira on it. I've got a yard full of material and I've paid for that, too. The Governor of Lagos Province says the work we are doing is the best they've ever had and I'm working now in a number of other provinces, too. But," and here he smiled, "I have bought a Mercedes. I paid cash for it, and I still have cash in the bank. And I do believe, in a couple of years, I've been looking around the island to find somewhere nice to live. I owe my success to you."

John said, "No, you don't. You owe it to yourself. You owe it to your own determination and your willingness to make the sacrifices now in order to have the rewards later on."

## 4. The willingness to take responsibility

Only one person is responsible for the success or failure of your business. You want to know who it is? Go and stand in front of the mirror. See that person looking back at you? That's the one. It's you. If your business is going to succeed, it will be because you made it. If your business fails, the failure will be down to you. Some people talk about economic downturns, government interventions, unfair competition, but those are excuses and one of the distinguishing marks of the successful business person is: the realization that they are where the buck stops. They don't make excuses. And neither should you be, because one of the distinguishing marks of the successful business person is: the realization that they are where the buck stops. They don't make excuses. If something goes wrong, they accept responsibility. And so they should, because when things go right they will also get the credit. They won't necessarily claim it, because one of the things successful business people do is to take blame themselves pass credit to other people to reward and encourage them, but people will know who is really responsible for the business's success.

All sorts of things can go wrong. You may have a best-selling product and the company that makes it is taken over by someone who regards you as a competitor and now the price they'll sell to you at is so high that you can no longer sell it as a profit. A completely new technology (this happens now with increasing frequency) may make the service or product you have been offering up to now outdated. An economic collapse of the sort we've seen a couple of times in the last few years may reduce the amount of money available for people to buy from you.

Well, tough. That's how it is. An entrepreneur's job is to meet the challenges as they arise and deal with them. Business winners know the responsibility is theirs and no-one else's, and they take it:

**"If it's going to happen, it will be me that makes it so."**

Don't print that and stick it on your office wall, because anyone who sees it will think you are very conceited person – but have it in your mind and repeated to yourself every day. Only one person carry responsibility for the success or failure of your business. That person is you.

## 5. An absolute commitment to success

There are no half measures in business. You can't stand on the high board, looking down at the pool and wondering what the water is like. Dive. Start swimming. Give it everything you have. You must be totally committed to success because, if you're not, you will fail.

If your situation means that you can't give up your day job until the business is fully established, you will have to work twice as hard so that you can give satisfaction in both jobs, because success demands your full attention.

## 6. A willingness to go the extra mile

Really, this follows from what I was just saying about doing two jobs at the same time. Going the extra mile is a well-known expression; what it means is that you don't set limits on what you're prepared to do. You may, however, set limits on what you promise.

Let's say that one of your customers needs delivery no later than next Tuesday. Today is Thursday. The current schedule for when you will have this product in stock would mean that you wouldn't get it there till next Wednesday. Clearly, that won't do. What normally happens with this product is that your supplier delivers it to you as part of one of their regular runs. You contact the supplier and the supplier says that, yes, they have it in stock and if necessary they could make an early delivery. They'd charge for that, but the amount of the charge will still leave you with a decent margin on the sale. You call the customer and say, yes, you can get it there for Tuesday. The customer places the order.

And now you weigh the alternatives. You've committed to deliver it on Tuesday, and you know you can do that, but you call the supplier and say, "If I wanted to collect it tomorrow, could you have it ready?" The supplier says, yes, no problem. The cost of sending your own driver is less than the additional charge the supplier would make for bringing it to you early, but that's not the only charge you have to consider: if you send your driver, other deliveries will slip, so you will have satisfied one customer by letting down another. Bad idea! Now you ring a transport company and they confirm they can collect it tomorrow, get it to you the same day, and charge no more than the supplier would – which is not surprising, given that is probably the solution that the supplier was planning to adopt. What, you ask, would be the charge to collect it from the supplier, deliver it to your customer with your paperwork, and mail the signed delivery note back to you? No difference, says the transport company.

So that's what you do. You go the extra mile. The customer wanted it by no later than Tuesday, you promised that would happen, but you delivered the previous Friday. Everyone's happy (you make sure of that by telephoning the customer and asking if a Friday delivery would be okay, because nothing would have been worse than getting it there and having it turned away because they weren't ready for it) and what the customer has seen is that you outperform your own promises.

Customers love that, they make you a preferred supplier and they come back for more. Which is why you were here successful business people with a long track record say that, "If you continually do more than you get paid for, the time will come when you are paid for more than you actually do."

Reciprocity is a basic element in normal human behavior. When you do something for someone, that someone feels an obligation to do something for you. They may not put it into words, but they feel it. Reciprocity is what makes going the extra mile such a successful business strategy.

Do be sure, though, that what you are doing really is "the extra mile." Expected standards of service are now so high that simply providing a very good service will not be enough, because that's what people expect. In the last few years, the world has moved from being fundamentally a seller's market to being a buyer's market. Do you remember those advertisements that used to talk about "delighting your customer"? You don't see those adverts any more, do you? The reason is that it's no longer possible to delight or amaze a customer simply by performing at 100% of the promised and/or expected service level, because 100% is what customers expect and they will no longer settle for less. For reciprocity to kick in, what you are doing for the customer really does have to be more than the maximum the customer could possibly have expected.


## 7. The ability to manage time effectively

Musicians know about time, because time is one of the key elements in music. When musicians talk about time, the words they use are things like, "beat," "interval," and "rest." If you're ever unfortunate enough to be at a concert where one or more of the musicians loses control of time, you'll know about it, because what should be one of life's greatest pleasures will have turned into a clashing cacophony. But you were never at a concert like that, because one of the first things musicians learn to manage is time.

And so must you.

You have 60 seconds in each minute, 60 minutes in each hour, and 24 hours in each day. Just the same as everyone else. If you want to be a successful business person, you can't get any more time – it just isn't for sale. What you have to do is manage the time you have. Regard it as an asset with a cash value. Be mean with it. Invest it in the projects that will show a good return, and don't squander it on vanity projects or things that lead nowhere.

## 8. They are determined and they are persistent

"When the going gets tough, the tough get going." It's a mark of successful people that they are determined to succeed and they keep going, whatever obstacles appear before them. Perhaps your competitors will cut their prices in an attempt to drive you out of the market. Perhaps they have launched a special campaign to get at your very best customers and woo them away from you. Perhaps it seems to be working.

That's when they'll find out what you are really made of. And so will you. Go back to the goals you set yourself and remind yourself that they are still your goals. Don't give up. Talk to your customers as though they were still your customers. And bear in mind that the single most important thing you can offer is quality of service.

A contracting company in Cyprus had always bought building materials from one specific company. George, the Managing Director, came under great pressure from one of that supplier's competitors who cut prices to the bone in order to drive George into their hands, and George was tempted, but his Operations Director said, "No." When George asked why, the answer was, "X has always been there for us, always gone that extra mile to make sure we got what we needed, always responded when we needed to know how to do something we hadn't done before. You can't throw away all that support just for money."

Bear that in mind when you are faced with price competition you simply can't meet. It isn't only about price. As I've already told you, service levels and going the extra mile are the most important things you can do in the long run. Before this chapter ends, I'm going to be talking about a business writer called Dale Carnegie. Here's something he said that everyone in business should have engraved on their hearts:

*Most of the important things in the world have been accomplished by people who have kept on trying when there seemed to be no hope at all.*

# To Personal Characteristics,
# Add Personal Competences

Those are the eight personal qualities that all successful business people have. To them, we can add six personal competences that you need to develop if you are to enjoy the maximum possible success:

## 1. Effective Communication

No-one gets anywhere at anything without being able to communicate effectively. And that does not simply mean being able to make your instructions clear (though, on occasion, that ability will be vital). Communication is not a one-way process. As well as speaking, you have to be able to listen, and as well as listening you have to be able to HEAR. And, no, listening and hearing are not the same thing. The best salespeople have been described as "two ears and one mouth, in that proportion." That description applies because listening, and understanding what you are hearing, are more important to a salesperson than – well, frankly, than anything else in the world.

One very important aspect of communication is that it has to be a matter of interaction, and that is what I mean when I talk about it being a two-way process. And good interaction occurs at all levels. You must be able to communicate with the guy on the gate as effectively as with the chairman of the board. Bear in mind that it may be unreasonable to expect the guy on the gate to understand an idea presented in the way you would present it to the chairman of the board, and vice versa. If you have a message to convey, express it in the terms that the person you are speaking to will understand.

And bear in mind that no two people are exactly the same. We all behave differently, and we all communicate differently, and what you need to do if you are to be successful is to pick out the communication style of the person you are dealing with, understand it and respond to it. Use their vocabulary, where possible, and not yours. Feel free to use the jargon of your industry to someone from within that industry, but use clearer terms when speaking to an outsider.

## 2. Not drifting off target

I've already had quite a lot to say about the need to be able to focus, and that is also what I'm talking about here. You have to be able to think on your feet and respond quickly when something is not going as it should, and to do that you have to be concentrating – focusing – otherwise, you won't spot that the target isn't where it was until it has moved too far for an easy correction. Be prepared to admit – certainly to yourself, and if necessary to other people – that you got it wrong. But, when you do get it wrong, see that you have got it wrong and fix the problem immediately. What's expensive is not making a mistake; it is one of these:

- Failing to notice that you've made a mistake
- Refusing to admit that you've made a mistake
- Not fixing your mistake while it is still fixable.

## 3. Foresight

I'm not talking about the ability to tell in advance which musician is going to win the Grammys this year, although that would be a very useful talent. What I am talking about is being able to see a trend early enough to take action. Somebody once said that, by the time most people have seen a bandwagon and jumped on it, its journey is already over. It's important for success in business to be able to see what trends and changes are emerging, but also what trends and changes may emerge in the next little while. You can do that to some extent by reading all the trade magazines and similar literature, and subscribing to email newsletters, but never forget that these are essentially crystal ball activities. The person saying, "This is what is going to happen," doesn't actually know for certain what is going to happen, any more than you do. It's informed speculation. Worse, such a story can sometimes be planted by a company with a vested interest in leading people the wrong way down a one-way street – one that turns into a dead end.

What is more important is to spend time thinking about how emerging trends are going to affect your business. Too many companies allow themselves to be paralyzed by worry about what's happening, or stick their heads in the sand and pretend they can't see it and, in any case, it will go away if they ignore it. As I've already said earlier, if you ignore a problem it does not go away; it gets worse.

## 4. Leadership

Anyone – or almost anyone – can persuade themselves to do something. Leadership is the ability to get others to do something. It's less common than it could be, and that presents an opportunity, because once you have analyzed a customer's problem and worked out a solution, your next task is to persuade the customer to adopt your recommendation. This is why selling is sometimes described as, "the gentle art of giving the other person your own way."

Your position as expert in the field – the professional – is what gives you the edge. The customer has asked for your help or your advice. Give it, and do not give it in a hesitant or uncertain way. Learn to present proposals as the most obvious way to go – create the idea that anyone who does not take your advice on this matter is risking disaster. And, if you are reluctant to do that, remind yourself that it's what the customer asked you to do.

## 5. Salesmanship

Some of the best sales people I know are women, but I refused to change that word to "salespersonship" because that would be about as ugly as a word can be. People sometimes look down on selling and sales people. I can guarantee that you have received phone calls from people you don't know who began with the words, "I'm not trying to sell you anything," when it's quite clear that selling you something is exactly what they are trying to do. The IBM salesman I mentioned earlier in this book always responds to that with the words, "Never speak those words to a salesperson," and hangs up. The reason people begin their call like that is because they think the person they are calling will have a dim view of salespeople. And that's crazy. Because no business has ever succeeded without the ability to sell. If you don't have that ability, I suggest you acquire it. Fast.

There's no need to go to great lengths; don't believe anyone who tells you that salespeople are born, not made. That's nonsense! Dale Carnegie went to The Great Sales Conference In The Sky half a century ago, but his book *How to Win Friends and Influence People* is still one of the best primers on salesmanship the world has to show. Why? Because it gets you to focus on the person you are selling to and that person's interests, needs, and trigger points – and that is what selling is. He summed it all up in this one line:

*You can make more friends in two months by becoming interested in other people than you can in two years by trying to get other people interested in you.*

And here's a little rule (not, this time, from Dale Carnegie) that you might like to remember:

*Just because you've told them, don't assume they know*

I was taught that rule by one of my clients. He told me this story. He sold computer equipment and peripherals and he had a number of customers who were very loyal to him and would not go anywhere else if he had what they needed. One day, he was visiting a long-standing customer who, over the years, had done large amounts of business with him. He showed them what he described as "a rather nice new device we had just developed." The IT director was sufficiently impressed that he asked for a demonstration of this device to the whole of the IT department and my client did that, but no sale came about at that time. A few months later, he got a call from the IT director. "X (one of my client's competitors at the time) has just shown me something rather neat." And then he described a device identical to the one my client had shown him a few months before. "Do you have anything like that?"

Now, my client could have said, "Yes, you damn fool, I do, and I showed it to you. Weren't you paying attention?" He could have said that. But saying things like that was not how he came to have so many good, loyal customers and get himself sent every year to 100% Clubs in lovely places in the first place. What he actually said was, "Yes, I do. Would you like me to bring one in and show it to you?" They agreed a date and when he got there the whole IT department was once again waiting for his demonstration.

As he describes the occasion, there was a certain amount of nudging and whispering as he went through his demonstration and people realized they'd seen it before, but he kept a straight face. This time, he got the order.

So bear that in mind. Your customers are busy people. Just because you've told them something, don't assume that they have kept the information in their heads. You told them once. Tell them again – as many times as you have to.

The object of salesmanship is not to sell as many products as you can. The object is to satisfy the customer's needs. Here's another rule about salesmanship that is well worth remembering:

### *If the prospect doesn't have a problem, you can't make a sale*

The reason for that rule is that every sale is a solution to a problem. Now, that word "problem" can have many meanings. You might wonder what sort of problem is being solved when someone buys a solid gold Rolex watch, given that watches are to be had at far lower prices, and some of those cheapo watches look rather nice. Well, it may be that the problem being solved is not simply that the buyer needs to be able to tell what time it is, but that she or he operates in an environment where it is necessary to demonstrate that you are well off and have a high level of disposable income.

What means in practice is that you need to spend some time analyzing what the prospect (a prospect is someone you may sell to in the future but haven't sold to yet, whereas a customer is someone you have already sold to) is really saying to you and what it really means. What you are looking for is the problem – the trigger – the thing that will make the prospect say, "I'll take it."


## 6. Action

I've left this one till last because, without it, the rest are wasted. You can know everything you need to know and have every skill the situation demands, but if you don't do anything, then what's the point of all that knowledge and all those skills? You know what you have to do.

### So do it.

*"There's nothing wrong with staying small. You can do big things with a small team"*

Jason Fried

# Principle 2

# What Image Do You Present To Customers?

## Managing The Way Customers See You

The word "professional" means different things to different people. A professional musician is someone who can make a living from music, and someone just starting out on the rocky road to musical success may look with longing at that person's life. Often, though, "professional" is used to describe a manner – the way someone presents herself or himself. For you, what really matters is what professionalism means to your customers, because you want them to see you as professional. The best way to achieve that is summed up in this one-liner:

**Focus on being the best you can at what you want to do**

I'm now going to talk about salesmanship again. If you're thinking, "Hey, I didn't sign up to a sales training course," that's okay, because I'm not planning on running one – but selling is at the heart of everything you do, and you need to take that on board. (It's also handy for you to understand something about how salespeople work – and what makes a good one – if you employ salespeople).

Before I get to that, however:

# Asking For The Order

The ability to ask for the order is crucial. A huge amount of business is lost simply because the moment when the prospect is ready to buy comes…and then it goes. The only reason the prospect doesn't place an order at that moment was…s/he isn't asked for it.

Now, you might say, "Look, if the guy is ready to buy, s/he'll buy. Right?" Sadly, the answer to that is often, "Wrong." Even when they're ready to buy, people like to be asked. If they're not asked, the moment of readiness can pass. Successful salespeople may ask for the order three times during a call. Not by saying "Please give me the order" each time – there are lots of ways to make that request without speaking those words. Asking for the order is a critical skill, and not every salesperson has it. Those who do will sell more – far more – than those who don't.

# Salespeople Come In Five Models

There are different kinds of salespeople. They work in different ways, have different skillsets, get results differently and see the job in different ways. As I go through the different types of salesperson, think about how they relate to salespeople you meet in the course of business and salespeople you employ.

Then think about how they relate to YOU.

## The Caller

Callers make appointments easily. The bit of the job they enjoy is meeting people and talking to them. They're not so good at the nitty-gritty: getting prospects/customers to talk about problems they may be having so that they can tell whether there's something there to which they have a solution – something that can lead to a sale. Nor do they often ask for the order.

Typically, callers' presentations are verbal; there's little use of brochures and other visual aids and they find producing formal proposals to be absolute torture.

## The League of Gentlemen Order Takers

Actually, order takers can also be women, but I love this expression that was coined by the ex-IBM salesman client I've mentioned before. He used it as a term of contempt, and it's possible to see why. Order Takers are passive. They don't ask for the order. They might pop in to a valued long-term customer (probably one they inherited from another salesperson) and say, "Anything for me today?" but that's as far as it will go.

They aren't good at making appointments, initiating contact, handling objections, cross-selling or selling higher value products and services. Their usual sales technique, if it deserves to be called that, is, "Give me a price and I'll get under it." If the customer has a problem that one of your products or services could solve, don't expect this salesperson to find out about it.

## The Hustler

This person wants the sale, and doesn't really focus on anything else. "That's good," you may say, and there are certainly a lot of them around (especially in tele-sales; you may very well have had one of these people on the phone this week. And last week. And the week before. And… It's also true that they get results, at least often enough to bring in enough business to keep their jobs; they may sometimes be high on the salespeople's leaderboard.

They have good product knowledge. What they may lack is people skills and, in particular, the sensitivity to "read" the prospect and react to what they find.

## The Problem Solver

What problem solvers enjoy most about the job is building empathy with the prospect or customer, asking detailed questions and understanding the answers, and feeling their way to a grasp of what the problem is and how to fix it. If they can combine that with the ability to ask for the order, especially if the product is in any way complex, they can be the company's premier salespeople. If not…well, it's great to know they understand the problem, but what they're actually there for is to bring home the bacon and what they're doing is condemning the company to a vegan existence.

## The Advisor

Advisors act as counsellors, offering advice and support. They can build rapport and empathy, no problem. Their written proposals are second to none, and the solutions they offer will work – if they wouldn't, the advisor would not suggest them. Customers recognize professionalism; they know that they are dealing with someone who cares about them and – so long as the advisor knows how to ask for the order – these are likely to be the company's best performers over any reasonably long stretch of time.

# To See Ourselves As Others See Us

The Scottish poet Robert Burns wrote:
O wad some Power the giftie gie us
To see oursels as ithers see us!
It wad frae mony a blunder free us

Burns was writing in the Scots-English dialect of the 18th century; translated into the English we understand today, those words mean:

*If only we had the power to see ourselves as others see us –*
*we would avoid so many blunders*

Hard to argue with that. So, how do your customers see you? Here are two common views customers have:

- You're a typical salesman, intent on taking an order above all else and concerned primarily with the commission you would earn
- You're interested in them, as a business and as people, and what you want is to make sure they receive the advice they need and end up with the products and services that will most effectively meet their needs

Which of these categories you fall into will play a large part in deciding how successful you are in business.

Customers who see you as falling into the second category – an advisor; someone with their interests at heart; someone who will help them understand

and solve their problems – they will welcome you into their offices, their factories, their homes (if you're a B2C business) and their hearts. THEY'LL WANT TO DO BUSINESS WITH YOU!

I trust that makes clear which image of yourself you want your customers to have.

## It Isn't Really About The Product

As humans, we like to think that we are all logical, reasoning beings. We are deluding ourselves. Perhaps not entirely – between three and four out of every 10 decisions to buy a product or service are made on logical grounds. The other six to seven have more to do with emotion and feelings than with logic. That 65% of buyers are buying because of the way they feel about the person they are buying from *and the way they believe that person feels about them.*

So stop trying to sell products and services to your customers and prospects, and start selling YOU and the feelings of warmth, security and confidence they get from dealing with you.

You may be able to ignore that advice if you are the only person in the world selling this product or service, and it is one the prospect or customer absolutely must have. And how many people in the world do you imagine fall into that category? And are you one of them? No, I thought not.

You might also want to look at these questions.

All of your competitors asking higher price than you are?

- Do none of them offer a better quality product?
- How about additional features and services – are they unavailable from any of your competitors?

  Once again, no, I thought not.

And when you look at it in those terms, your first reaction may be: "Then I'm completely wasting my time trying to sell anything to anybody." And I understand why you would feel that – but you're wrong. Understand that, in the globally connected world we live in today, everyone's offer is on view to everyone else. You're never going to be the person offering the lowest price/highest quality/ maximum number of additional features/whatever – so stop trying. Instead, major on the one thing you do have that no one else on the planet can offer. YOU!

I was talking the other day to a freelance graphics designer. She charges $80 an hour, and she competes with people prepared to go down to $10 an hour. And yet, her workload is always at full capacity, and she regularly turns work away, while some of those $10 competitors are lucky to fill two days a week. Why is that? Here's her answer: "I always have a full schedule because people want me to do the job for them and not someone else." And why do they want that? "Well, if you look at the testimonials on my website, you'll see there's general agreement that I take time to understand what is required, and I'm like a chameleon – whatever the "voice" and the "style" of the customer may be, they find that I match it."

So there's someone charging eight times what some of her competitors charge, and still hitting 100% of her target, while competitors struggle.

That's the lesson I want you to take away from this part of this chapter. It isn't about the product and it isn't about the service. It's about the person who delivers that product or service. What you have to focus on is selling your expertise, your knowledge, and your ability to empathize with the customer, together with one more thing: your desire to solve the customer's problem by delivering what the customer needs.

Note that word, "desire." I recommend my clients not to use expressions like, "We are passionate about…" followed by whatever it is they are selling. It might be coffee, it might be programming, it might be providing a rent guarantee service to landlords, but whatever it is, you can bet your sweet bippy that a lot of people in that industry are claiming to be passionate about it. And that's the reason I recommend that my clients not use it – because it has become so common that people not only discount it, but have begun to ridicule it. Nevertheless, whether you name it or not, passion is something that you have to show. And if you do, and if prospects see it, you won't need to compete on price. People will be lining up to pay whatever you ask in order to get the thing they want most of all – YOU.

## Which of the two are you?

It isn't hard to decide which of the two categories – advisor or hard sell merchant – your customers put you into, because they tell you. Not in words, but in what they call on you for. So monitor it. Every time you receive an email, make a customer visit, take a telephone call – any time you have any contact at all from prospects and customers – make a note. (You're doing that, anyway, right? Because, if you're not, get yourself a CRM program RIGHT NOW and start; you can't plan how to meet your targets and monitor your progress unless you track every single contact with a customer or prospect to see where it goes and to analyze how you could have handled it better). What I'm asking you to do is to add one question to that CRM record: Was the purpose of the inquiry to ask your advice or help? (If so, you were an advisor). Or was it to get a quote for a possible order? (If so, you were a seller).

Tot up the number of answers in each category at the end of each month and you'll know how your customers see you. And, if you're clearly seen more as a seller than as an advisor, you have some hard work ahead of you, because you have to change that perception.

*"if you don't do it excellently, don't do it at all. Because if it's not excellent, it won't be fun or profitable, and if you're not in business for fun or profit, what the hell are you doing here?"*

Robert C Townsend

# Principle 3

# Fixing Your Own Value

## How to know your worth, and how to increase it

The first thing I want you to accept in this chapter is that you have to regard yourself as a standalone business. That's true if you are a one-person trading entity, selling things on eBay, and it's true if you are a junior employee of a company employing 50,000 people on five continents – you are still in business for yourself. And the object of that business is to increase your earnings.

Now, listen. Before you get into a tizz, I did not say that was the only object. Sure, there are lots of others – enjoying life, having enough time to see friends and family, the occasional break when you can just lay back and relax without a care in the world. They're all important. But increasing your earnings comes first, because it, generally, is what makes the other things possible. And it's how you keep score of your own progress. You do want to progress, don't you?

I've heard all those stories about money not buying happiness. I've also heard what Michael Caine had to say about that: "The idea that money can't buy happiness is a lie told by the rich to stop you shooting them."

And here, as far as I'm concerned, is the clinching argument:

- If you are self-employed, if you don't make enough money, you'll go bankrupt and be out of work;
- If you work for someone else, unless you make enough money for them (through selling things, cutting costs, building a more reliable product – whatever your particular line of work happens to be), then either they will fire you or their business will fail. Either way, you'll still be out of work.

So, if you don't already, start seeing yourself as a business that stands or falls on the number of dollars you generate.

## Three Secrets Of Success

There's an old British saying, "You can't make a silk purse out of a sow's ear." (A sow, in case you haven't come across the word, is a female pig). That expression has been around for 400 years; it was first used by an English clergyman in 1579 when he wrote, "Seeking to make a silk purse out of a sow's ear." He was describing people engaged in a task that couldn't be done. And, since we're talking about things that can't be done, I'll quote here a little rhyme that also comes from England, or at least that I first heard from an English correspondent:

*They told me the job just couldn't be done*
*So I went right to it*
*I tackled the job that couldn't be done*
*And I couldn't do it.*

Why, when I'm so keen to motivate you to great things, am I talking about things that can't be done? Because they exist, and you'll go further faster if you recognize them for what they are and avoid them.

Here are the three secrets for success:

1. There has to be a need for what you offer. (Notice that I don't say there has to be a "demand" – it may be up to you to create demand – but there must be a need)

2. You must be able to do it
3. It must be sufficiently difficult to replace you that people will want to pay your price

Think of the difference in take-home pay between Jennifer Lawrence ($46 million last year) and – say – a burger flipper in MacDonalds. Jennifer Lawrence starred in *Hunger Games*, which has grossed $653.4 million at the box office (so far; it isn't over yet). Those numbers themselves indicate the demand for the product, and Jennifer Lawrence has a reputation for turning up and doing the job without difficulty – she's no prima donna – so that takes care of requirement 2. The producers will have made a cold-eyed calculation of how many tickets she would sell compared with other female stars they could offer the part to and concluded that, while she could be replaced, it would not be easy and any replacement they considered might very well not fill as many seats. Those are the reasons for her phenomenal income (which, amazingly, was actually about $7 million *down* on the previous year).

And the burger flipper? Well, looking at typical salaries in Kentucky, the state in which Jennifer Lawrence was born, you're looking at less than $20,000 a year. In fact, it can be as low as $15,000. We know the demand for burgers is certainly there, so why isn't the pay higher? Work through the three criteria and you'll see why. Yes, the demand for burgers is there. And we know the person doing the job can do it, because almost anyone can do it. And if one of them leaves? How long do you think it would take that particular restaurant to find a replacement? Ten minutes?

I know it's harsh, but those are the reasons why one person can earn enough that they need never work again, even if they live three lifetimes, and another works hard day after day and has almost nothing left after paying the rent on a not-very-good one-room apartment.

## Raising Your Market Value

Somewhere between those two extremes of $46 million and $15,000 is you. You know where you are on the scale, and I would not be so rude as to ask; what I will do is to make some suggestions on moving your value towards the higher end.

Here are two rules to take to heart:

*Top level earnings are only paid to top level people*
and

*Top level people are those who provide a top level service or product*

That's capitalism. It's how the free market works. If you only do what others do, you can only expect to be paid what others earn.

But, hey, isn't that a problem? We've already seen that global networking means goods and services everywhere are fairly similar in price and quality, so how do you stand out?

In fact, I've already answered that when I talked about the freelance graphic artist. People pay her eight times what they pay other people, and keep her busy for every hour she's prepared to spend at work – why? Because of the superior service she offers – the way she understands exactly what her customers need *and delivers it*. The same reasons, in fact, as the ones that motivated the *Hunger Games* producers to reward Jennifer Lawrence so lavishly.

It's a question of added value; the value you add to your customers is rewarded by the increase in your own value.

So that's where you focus your attention.

## Generating Success

Question: Is there a great need for what you do? If not, perhaps you should consider doing something else.

Second, related, question: Is there a great demand for what you do? If not, but you have determined that there is a need, then you had better get to work to create the demand. Because saying that there's a need for something, but no demand, means that people have not been made aware that a product or service exists to meet a need they have. The product or service is yours, so creating that awareness is down to you.

Assuming (as will usually be the case) that both need and demand already exist, you need to get cracking. And one of the first things you have to do is:

### *Qualify Your Prospects*

A qualified prospect meets the following criteria:

- S/he needs your product or service and knows that s/he needs it – i.e. wants it (that criterion establishes that both need and demand are there)
- S/he can afford to pay for it
- You are talking to someone with authority to make a buying decision (a decision-maker)

John, the ex-IBM salesman I have mentioned before, developed a rather neat method of rating prospects from 20% to 100%. He's given me permission to show it to you. He says that, until all points in Stage 1 are met, you don't have a prospect at all; what you have is what he calls a "suspect":

| Stage | Criteria | %age prospect |
|-------|----------|---------------|
| 1 | 1. The prospect has a problem, and knows that the problem exists<br>2. You have what may be a solution to the prospect's problem<br>3. The prospect acknowledges that you may have a solution | 20% |
| 2 | You carry out a full evaluation of the problem, with the prospect's approval and co-operation | 40% |
| 3 | **Key stage in the process**<br>A prospect decision-maker agrees to invest the prospect's time and the prospect's resources in evaluating your solution | 60% |
| 4 | The prospect places an order | 80% |
| 5 | 1. You have delivered the product or service ordered<br>2. The customer has paid you<br>3. 5 days have passed and the check has not bounced | 100% |

At the time I'm speaking of – qualifying the prospect – stage 5 is still a long way off. The reason you need to qualify a prospect is to make sure you're not wasting your time in trying to sell something to someone who:

- Doesn't need it;
- Doesn't want it (regardless of need);
- Can't afford to buy it; *or*
- Doesn't have the authority to place an order.

In their early days, most salespeople are reluctant to stop talking to a suspect who meets any of those four bullet points because "it would seem rude." You can tell the mature salesperson because they're the ones who have discarded that approach and are ruthless in ending conversations with people who are not going to buy from them – and equally ruthless in hanging in there when the prospect is reluctant to place an order but the salesperson knows all the criteria are met.

### *Delivering*

You don't get paid for what it says in your job description. You get paid for what you do and how well you do it. I could go on about this, but I'm not going to because it seems to me to be obvious: what determines how well you do and how much you are paid is not what responsibilities you may or may not have, but how well you perform them.

### *Replaceability*

This is the final factor I set down in determining your financial rewards. It's not about what you are worth as a human being – that would be demeaning. It's about the value you add to the business and – in this third case – how easy the business would find it to replace you with someone else who offered at least equal added value.

But, you may say, in my case I AM the business. Okay; then for you it's not a matter of how easy you would find it to replace yourself with someone adding the same value, but how easy your customers would find it to replace you as a supplier.

Walt Disney (and there's a man who knew what it meant to be successful) summed all of this up extremely well in what he called his Law of Unlimited Abundance:

**"Do what you do so well that the people who see you do it will want to see you do it again, and will bring others to see you do it."**

So that's what you must focus on. "Do what you do" means, do what YOU do. There's a great deal of evidence to say that the first business in a new field establishes an advantage that lasts a very long time and is difficult to overcome. If you decide to be a "me-too," offering something that lots of other people offer, you will find it more difficult to sell other than on price than if you introduced something completely new. But the something completely new can be an improved standard of something that has been done before. What you are seeking is something specific to you – something that makes you stand out so the people want you as a supplier, and no one else.

That – this business of setting a new standard – is what Disney meant when he talked about doing what you do so well and people will want to see you do it again and they'll bring others to see you do it.

# Cast Your Bread Upon The Waters. But Make Sure It's Good Bread

Whatever your reasons for going into business for yourself, they are probably fundamentally selfish: a wish to be free, to be your own boss, not to have to answer other people, to get away from the decisions of people for whom you lack respect. Selfish or not, there's nothing wrong with those reasons, but they are not enough. The most important thing you need is an understanding the best way to meet *your* needs is to meet *the customer's* needs. The company or person you're selling to wants the very best for themselves. And giving it to them is, perhaps amazingly, the best way to get the very best for YOU.

In the long run (and, in fact, the not-so-long run), what all this boils down to is that it may be your employer who signs your paycheck, but it isn't your employer who pays you. It's the customer.

If you take nothing else away from this book, take that.

*"When obstacles arise, you change your direction to reach your goal; you do not change your decision to get there."*

Zig Zigler

# Principle 4

# Reasons For Buying

## What Makes A Customer Want To Buy?

Think about all the things people buy. Cars, washing machines, watches, document shredders… The list is endless. And there are services as well as products: insurance, gutter cleaning, dog walking… Once again, the list goes on and on.

These things that people buy. I don't think there's a single case – and, if there are such cases, they are very few – where the person wants the thing or service they have bought. And, when I say that, I can hear the shouts of objection. Why would anyone buy something they don't want? But it's a fact: most things (if not quite all) are not bought by people who want them. What those buyers want is the benefit that comes from the thing they buy.

I mentioned cars. All right, I know there are people who get excited about the shape and appearance of some cars, but there are very, very few automobiles (if any) that you would buy for purely aesthetic reasons. I mean, look at them! Great big things, sitting on your driveway, blocking out the light, needing to be washed regularly, and subject to government demands that you pay to insure them. And then there's depreciation; with every day that goes by, your investment in the car (unless it is a classic car) loses a little of its value. Why would anybody want such a thing?

And the fact is that most people don't. What they want is to be able to get from one place to another quickly and conveniently. They want to be able to take with them the luggage or other equipment that this particular trip requires without their arms being ripped from the sockets. In other words, they want the benefits that come from owning a car and to have those benefits they are prepared to saddle themselves with the thing and all the negatives that go with it.

It will be the same with whatever it is that you sell, which is why I talked some time ago about selling the sizzle and not the steak. And if that is not an excellent example of what I'm talking about, I don't know what would be. Why does anyone buy a steak? It certainly can't be for the thing itself – just tell yourself that someone wants to buy a steak for the sake of owning a chunk of dead animal flesh and you'll see how ridiculous that is. You don't have to be a vegetarian to find the very idea repellent. No, when someone buys a steak what they are buying is the pleasure of smelling it as it cooks and the at least equal pleasure of tasting it when it's done.

## Sell The Sizzle, Not The Steak (Reprise)

Since people don't want the thing or service that you are selling, don't waste time trying to sell it to them. Work out what it is that people buy for, and sell that. If you don't really know why people buy it, ASK them! I don't mean, "Why did you buy this thing from me?" because you don't want to cause them to ask themselves, "Why indeed?" and try to return it. Carry out a survey: ask your customers to list the five chief benefits they found in the purchase.

Now you have the basis on which you will construct your sales campaign. Let's talk about some of the more obvious reasons for buying something.

## Why People Buy

We have an advantage here, because psychologists have spent a great deal of money and a great deal of time examining the sometimes odd reasons why people do things – and that includes reasons for buying something. These reasons fall into seven categories.

## 1. The profit motive

If you sell something that the buyer can resell at a profit, you are offering a very good reason to buy. The desire to earn money is deep rooted. And that also works for things that will not themselves be sold on, but that will make it easier for your customers to run their business at a profit. It can be very simple: suppose you offer a form of packaging that means every time they make a sale they will earn a little more money than they did previously because it costs that much less to wrap whatever it is they are selling. No salesperson worthy of the name in a situation like that would even think of selling packaging (in the sense of saying, "Would you like to buy some packaging?") What they would sell is the extra profit that comes from the saving: "Boost your profits! Cut your costs! Packaging as reliable as always at lower cost!"

## 2. Fear

Fear is why people buy burglar alarms, smoke detectors, outdoor CCTV cameras. It's also how insurance companies survive, because no one wants to buy insurance but everyone wants to know that the disaster of a loss will be covered. And then there's life insurance, and medical insurance. People who sell these things focus their sales campaigns, their advertising and their patter on such things as: "Just imagine your husband's situation if he has to leave work to look after the children after something happens to you. Think of the dire poverty they'd end in. Is it fair to expose your loved ones to that risk? Especially the children?" Or: "There's more violence around today than there used to be, and criminals are less concerned about hurting people because they know the law doesn't deal with them as firmly as once it did. What installing these locks gives you is a level of safety inside your home greater than has ever previously been possible."

But don't waste your time pointing out the quality of the brass on the lock, the intricate chasing on the key, or the elegant printing on the insurance policy. No one is going to shell out good money for something like that.

## 3. Status

Early in this book, I invited you to consider what might motivate someone to buy a solid gold Rolex watch when a perfectly adequate timepiece is available for a fraction of the price. It's possible to go a little astray on this one, because the answer to the question: Why do people buy a watch? is, at first glance, so that they will know what time it is and not miss important appointments, and you don't need to spend several thousand dollars to achieve that. In fact, and especially among young people, the need to buy a watch is disappearing, because most people carry around a cell phone or more sophisticated device like a smartphone, and all they need to find out what time it is, is to look at that. And it will almost certainly have an alarm function, making it even less likely that they will miss an appointment. And yet watches go on selling. The reason for that has something to do with the comfort of doing what you've always done (wearing a watch) and the fact that a lot of watches look extremely attractive – they can be a fashion accessory. But that is not why people buy solid gold Rolexes. They do that because they want people to know they have "made it;" that they have made enough money and they don't mind splashing out what would be an annual food budget for some families on something to put on their wrist.

If you are selling something that can be seen as a status symbol, then forget about selling the object itself and go to town on selling the status.

It doesn't end there; you can sell particular types of bicycle to young boys (it's a parent that pays, but it's the boy that makes the choice) and particular types of smartphone to teenage girls (the same thing applies, but in this case it's the girl who makes the choice) by trading on the fact that some brands and some models have enormous status among their peers and some have none.

## 4. The Desire For An Easier Like

Whether you are aware of it or not, the desire to make life easier is part of us all. If you question that, count the number of labor-saving devices in your home. Got a dishwasher? Washing machine? Vacuum cleaner? What are they, if not ways to make life easier?

Is there anything about the products or services you sell that can make life easier for someone? If there is, that's one of the benefits you need to be pushing hard. Not necessarily the only one, because – for example – dishwashers bring the benefit of greater hygiene as well as saving effort, because they can withstand water at a much higher temperature than your hands can, but the ability to reduce the time or effort someone has to invest in a job is a big selling point and you should use it. When Adobe introduced PageMaker so many years ago it was the first desktop publishing software and the big buyers in the early days were not home users but people like magazine publishers. The reason they invested so heavily was that PageMaker made it possible for their layout artists to try out seven or eight alternative page layouts in the time it would previously have taken to do one. Magazines became more attractive in appearance as a result.

## 5. Excitement and Pleasure

Let's be frank about this: there is a pleasure that comes from owning something new. When you were young, it might have been a new pair of trainers. In your later teen years, a powerful gaming PC would have done the trick for quite a lot of people. As an adult, it could be a house of a sort and in a place that, once, you would have thought you could never afford.

People may not get much pleasure out of owning things, but they get an awful lot out of acquiring them. We are back to "Sell the sizzle, not the steak." Is it possible to have in your sales literature pictures of smiling people who have just taken delivery of something you sell? Stuff like that sells an awful lot of product. But use it with discretion. A picture of someone smiling as she boards an aircraft for her very first holiday without her parents? Of course. A similar picture illustrating the purchase of a bag of kitchen rolls? Somehow, it doesn't have the same oomph.

## 6. Self Improvement

An awful lot of training courses are bought because of mankind's almost insatiable desire to know more, to do things better, and to be better informed. You can build on that if you can produce real-life stories of people who have used what you offer to improve their businesses, their lives, their conversation, their social life – anything, in fact, that can be improved.

## 7. The Need For Acceptance

I had a prospect who told me that his brother-in-law had described him as, "The only person I ever met who really doesn't care what anyone else thinks of him." This prospect was really proud of that. I felt sorry for him. The need for acceptance begins in earliest childhood and, for almost everyone other than this prospect, never ends. I'm absolutely not saying that anyone should change what they really believe in to win approval from other people; what I am saying is that you should examine everything you sell, asking yourself the question: "Is there anything about this product or service that will help those who buy it feel a greater sense of acceptance?"

One of the ways this may show itself is when a parent does something for their spouse or children. They do it out of love, but – and this may be subconsciously – they want the fact that they have done it to be acknowledged. How can you take advantage of that? Well, you could have a place on your website (and, better still, on your Facebook page) that allows people to post remarks about things they have received or that have been done for them.

# Don't Take Your Customers For Granted

A study of the psychological characteristics such as the one we've just gone through should make this clear: customers need to feel valued. Add to the fact, as I said earlier, that only about 35% of the buying decision has to do with price and the rest is about feelings and you will see how important it is not to take your customers for granted. It's very easy to assume that, once won, a customer is yours for life. Easy – but wrong.

I don't suppose there's a single business anywhere in the developed world that has never lost a customer. (Of course, I exclude organizations like electricity generators and telephone companies – provided that there is the only one in a country, which is increasingly unusual – because their customers are captive and have nowhere else to go). Most businesses, though, have lost customers from time to time and will lose more.

That does not mean you should take it as a fact of life. If you lose a customer, try to get them back. Better still, stay in such close touch with your customers that they will be much less likely to leave you in the first place.

Accept that your competitors are going to try to take your customers away from you. Why wouldn't they? You're trying to take theirs from them (or, at least, I sincerely hope you are). That means staying aware of developments in your industry so that you see a threat coming. If someone has developed a new product or a new technique, find out as much about it as you can and think carefully about which customers they could attack with that product or technique and how you can combat it. And do that in advance – don't wait until the damage has been done.

Ways to stay close to your customer include:

- Newsletters. Make them regular and make them interesting. And be subtle about it, but make sure that each newsletter contains something to remind every customer of their reasons for becoming your customer in the first place
- Workshops. Invite customers to send their staff to you for training sessions. Apart from the direct benefit they'll receive, they'll find the opportunity to share with each other new ways they have found of using your product or service a real bonus.
- Visits. If you're selling the kind of product that requires customer visits to make the sale, keep those visits going afterwards. Check on how your product is performing, and whether they have any problems with it – and, once again, reinforce their reasons for buying from you

Companies who adopt that sort of approach lose far fewer customers than companies that don't.

*"Every sale has five basic obstacles: no need, no money, no hurry, no desire, no trust."*

Zig Zigler

# Principle 5

# Why Are We Here?

## It's About Profitability

At the head of Chapter 3, I quoted one-time Chairman of Avis Rental Cars Robert C Townsend as saying, "If you're not in business for fun or profit, what the hell are you doing here?" It's a very good question, but the fact is that very few people are sufficiently wealthy to be able to stay in business for fun alone. In the case of most businesses, if they are not making a profit, they are doomed.

What you need, then, is the ability to win and hold on to customers who will not only do repeat business with you (because repeat business is more profitable than one-off business) but also tell other people how marvelous you are and that they should be doing business with you, too (referrals). Sounds like a lot? Well, it may be, but it still isn't enough, because not only do you need to do those things, but you need to do them PROFITABLY.

Get that in place and you can look forward to a successful business career. Fail, and you can't. It really is that simple.

So how do you put yourself in that position?

# Winning Good Customers Profitably

A joke heard for countless years in countless companies across the globe runs, "Customers! Wouldn't life be easier without them!" It is a joke, and the reason it's a joke is that a business without customers cannot survive. If you don't have them, and have enough of them, you'd better go out and win some quickly or you're going to be shutting up shop.

But take a look again at that heading at the top of this section. It doesn't say, "Winning Customers Profitably." It specifies the kind of customer you want to win – GOOD customers.

Good customers are customers who:

*   Don't make dealing with them difficult
*   You can sell to at an acceptable profit
*   Repeat – they come back for more again and again
*   Provide referrals by recommending you to others

That's the kind of customer you want.

And now look at the fourth word in that heading: Profitably. There's no point winning customers if it costs you more to make the win than you're going to earn from the customer. That just brings failure a little bit closer. There's always an investment in winning a new customer. It may simply be the time it takes to send an email, and it may be the cost of setting up a protracted sales campaign, hiring a hotel room so that you can put on a seminar, travel and accommodation costs for several customer visits, and equipment rental. Whichever end of the scale is involved, you need to see a positive return on investment (ROI). Otherwise, it was a mistake to win the customer in the first place.

Once you've got the customer, your next step is to extract the maximum possible return from that customer. Like everything else in this book, that involves work.

Start by finding out as much as you possibly can, not just about the needs the customer had that were satisfied by a purchase from you, but ALL the customer's needs. Is there anything else you can sell to this customer to meet those needs? If not, do you have any contacts you can introduce the customer to who can solve those problems? If so, be sure to do it, because helping customers in that sort of way makes them feel good about you and reinforces their decision to deal with you in the first place and their willingness to stay with you in the future.

Okay, you've won your new customer and you're selling every product and service to them that you possibly can. You're not done yet. The next step is to look for referrals.

## Making Your Customers Your Salesforce

The word most commonly used to describe customers who tell other people nice things about you is, "Advocate." You want advocates; they can do far more good for you than your sales people. When a customer becomes an advocate, there are two advantages. The first is that they have bought from you in the past, which takes care of the trust issue always present in a decision to buy. What people who aren't yet customers will think is, "Well, those people over there bought one and they seem to be happy, so the product must be okay." A satisfied customer is the most powerful sales aid you can have. The second advantage is that prospects know that your sales people work for you, and so they expect them to say how wonderful you and your products are and, to at least some extent, they will discount that praise. When a customer says it, it does not have that same negative connotation and a customer's recommendation will be taken at face value.

So how do you get advocates? It's a lot easier than it used to be, because now we have websites and social marketing. Make sure there's somewhere on your website for customers to post testimonials. Then make sure some of them do, by asking them to! Set that page up so that all comments have to be approved before they can appear, and don't be shy about deleting without approval anything you don't like. Each time you get a good testimonial, tweet it and post it on your Facebook page.

And now let me take a moment or two out to address those who are reading this and thinking, "But I don't have a web page. I don't have a Twitter account. I don't have a Facebook page." It's the 21$^{st}$ Century! What on earth do you think you're doing? As soon as you finish this book, get started on setting up your web page, Twitter account and Facebook page. And if you don't know how to do that in a professional way, hire someone who does. If you don't have all three of those aids to marketing, you are missing out on an awful lot of sales.

As well as asking for online endorsements, ask customers when you visit them or speak to them on the phone if there is anyone they can think of to whom they might like to give a recommendation to buy your products. When people buy online you don't meet them in person, so offer a discount, or some other benefit, in return for a referral that turns into an order. (A quick note here: free delivery is not a suitable benefit to offer because, wherever possible, free delivery should be part of the deal you offer. Research by Econsultancy shows that 55% of online shoppers abandon their baskets at the moment when they discover they are going to be asked to pay for delivery. That's slightly more than half of your prospects who will not go on to buy because you want to charge them for delivery. So, if you possibly can, double your sales by including delivery in the price and advertising delivery as free. It's a no-brainer).

A step on the way to turning customers into advocates is turning one-time customers into repeat buyers. And that means holding onto the information you have about them, analyzing what you know about them, and working out offers likely to attract them. But take care, because the number of countries with legislation penalizing companies that don't remove customers from their mailing lists when asked to do so is large and growing. And, whatever you do, don't sell your customer contact details to anyone else. Customers hate that more than almost anything.

# Cross-sell. Sell more value. But Above All, Retain

Once you have a customer, do everything you can to sell them other products and services (cross-sell) and sell them higher value products. Most important of all, don't let them go.

Winning a new customer costs more than holding onto one you've already got. It follows that you want to keep your customers for as long as you possibly can. Cost is not the only reason; if you won an account away from a rival, you would tell the world about it (and, if not the world, you'd certainly make sure your prospects knew – especially those who still dealt with the rival in question), and you can be sure that the competitor to whom you lose an account will do the same.

In Chapter 6, I'll have some more to say about the true costs of losing a customer. For now, let's just focus on some of the things you need to do to protect your customer base against poachers:

- Take the trouble to know what is going on in your industry. Who is cutting prices? What new technology may be threatening the market for your product or service? Then work out your strategy for dealing with this new threat before it starts to damage you
- Stay in touch with customers. Use newsletters, seminars, social media and your website. Build a mailing list with a service such as MailChimp – they are good because they won't let you infringe on customers' rights
- Track every cross sell and higher value sale that happens. Talk to the customer in question and find out what use they are making of the additional product or service. Then use that story (of course, with the customer's permission) in a newsletter, blog post or similar (and, ideally, both) to get the message out to your other customers
- Be aware of the average length of time your customers take between purchases. If any of them exceed that time by more than 30%, send them a message. It could be an offer; it could be a "We miss you" message, but be careful of offers because customers soon work out that, if they delay the next purchase by a certain period of time, they'll get a better deal. So vary the nature of your contact. It isn't necessary always to offer something; often, the mere fact that you cared enough to get in touch will be enough.

*"You are what you do, not what you say you'll do."*

C G Jung

# Principle 6

# Grow Your Business In Four Steps

## Note: I didn't say easy steps.
## They're not. But they are essential

It's possible that there may be people who read the title of this chapter and think, "But I don't want to grow my business. I like it as it is. It's just the right size." And that's a mistake. Easy to understand, but a mistake. Because the one thing a business will not do is remain the same size. It either grows or it shrinks.

Take a look at your customers. Can you put your hand on your heart and say for certainty, "Not one of those will ever leave me"? You can't; if nothing else, the Grim Reaper will carry every one of them off at some point. But your competitors are trying all the time to find new ways to prize your customers out of your grip, and however hard you work, they are not going to fail every time with every single customer. So, if you want a long-term future, you do have to think about growing your business.

In any case, more is almost always better because some of your costs are fixed and, the more transactions you have to spread them across, the more profitable each transaction is. It's also worth remembering that, however much accountants may like to talk about the differences between fixed and variable costs, in the short term all costs are fixed.

# Build Your Customer Base

Did you notice what I said in that last paragraph? Or what I didn't say? I did not say, "the more customers you have to spread them across, the more profitable each customer is." I used the word "transaction" instead of customer because getting more customers is not the only way to build your business. Increasing the number of sales you make, and increasing the value of each sale you make, are two other ways to grow your business. I'm starting, though, with getting more customers. Here are some of the more common ways to do it

- Advertising – newspapers, TV, radio, cinemas
- Mailshots. Postcard marketing is particularly effective right now. A lot of businesses seem to have abandoned it as old hat, but those who are still using it report that results are as good as they were in the postcard's heyday. Email can work in certain markets, but be careful not to break the rules and make sure you remove immediately from your mailing list anyone who asks you to. And be aware that the email address lists generally on sale are mostly worthless
- Flyers. These can out through the mail, be delivered into people's mailboxes by hand, or go as inserts in a magazine or newspaper
- Online:
  o Pay-Per-Click (PPC), including but not limited to Google Adwords
  o Using social media (Twitter, Facebook, LinkedIn, Pinterest and the rest) to drive people to your website, where the products or services are offered. If using this approach, make sure you have good analytics – Google Analytics, Clicky Analytics – so that you know what is working and what is not. Unless this is your own expert field, get professional help

- Referrals from existing customers
- Telephone soliciting. Be very careful about this one, because it offends a lot of people and if they associate you with it you can be pretty sure they won't do business with you when you contact them in some other way. There are agencies who will do this for you; take care to speak to some of their customers first, because some agencies will do it with sensitivity, as you would wish, and some will not

Something that happens quite a lot is that, having decided to start advertising in order to boost their business, a company looks around at what everybody else in the industry is doing and does the same. The reason for this, presumably, is an assumption that, if the rest of the industry is doing that kind of advertising, that must be the right kind of advertising for the industry.

That is a very questionable form of logic. I would say that there is at least a 50/50 chance (and it may well be more) that choosing a different approach entirely will pay dividends. People are used to being canvassed in a particular way by businesses like yours, and when we become used to something we tend not to notice it. So, if you find – to take an example at random – that most of your competitors advertise through telephone solicitation, try something different. Flyers, for example.

And here is an idea that some of my clients have found very valuable. Forget about the kind of advertising your industry seems to do. What kind of advertising is working for OTHER businesses in OTHER industries?

Take a look. If you see something that seems to be working in an industry that's nothing like yours, maybe it would work in your industry, too. And yours would be the only business in your industry using it.

Get in touch with the company in a different industry that has an ad you like and ask them how they do it. Asking your own competitors for tips about effective advertising (or anything else to do with running a successful business in your marketplace) is likely to be counter-effective. Why would they tell you how to compete against them more effectively? But asking someone in a totally different line of business can be much more successful. First, they are pleased and flattered that you picked out what they were doing as an example of something good. And then, provided there is no cost to them (like lost business, which could ensue from advising a competitor) most people are happy to share information. Ask what agency they used, how they set the parameters, how much involvement they had… Ask anything you want to know.

## Value selling and Cross Sell

By value selling, I mean getting bigger orders from the same customer, it also call upsell. If you have 100 customers, and each one of them currently spends $1200 a month with you, just think what the impact on your bottom line would be if you could get that $1200 up to $1300 a month. You just made an extra $10,000 a month in revenue, so if your net margin is – say – 10%, you increased your bottom line profit by $12,000 a year. Now suppose you could get the $1200 a month up to $1500 a month.

It won't happen by accident. The best way to do it is to have a range of products at different prices. With new customers, focus on attracting them to the lowest cost product in the range, because that may very well be the easiest to sell the first time. After they've bought it, don't run it down – congratulate them on a wise purchase and stay in touch to make sure they are getting as much benefit as they can from it. While you're doing that, just be sure to let them know about the extra benefits that come from higher-featured products further up the range.

Many businesses have found that this is the easiest way there is to increase their revenue and their bottom line profit. No reason why you should not be the same.

Perhaps you only have one product in that range, in which case selling a higher value product is not going to be an option. Unless, however, that product is the only one you sell, you can still try cross selling, which is the term used for getting existing customers to buy a wider range of your products.

The first reason for doing this is that, the more products a customer buys from you, the less easy it will be for a competitor to take that customer away. And the second is that the easiest person to sell to is the person you have sold to before. They bought one of your products or services, they liked it – they are obvious candidates to buy another of your products or services.

But I said something there that may not be relevant. "They liked it." What if they didn't like it? Well, now, here is one of the most interesting things that all salespeople learn sooner or later:

### *The easiest person to sell to is someone you have sold to before –*
### *EVEN IF THE SALE WAS NOT AN UNCONDITIONAL SUCCESS*

If anything is counterintuitive, it's that. Most people who've never sold for a living like to stay away from people when something has gone wrong, because they think they'll get a pasting. Don't be like those people. Of course, if something went wrong with the original purchase, I'm assuming you did the things you should have done to put things right and didn't just wash your hands of the customer, the product and the problem. If you did those things, you scored some brownie points and at least you should expect a guarded welcome from the customer, even if there is a doubt there about buying from you again. However, it's a fact that even someone whose purchase was not entirely successful, if they have bought from you before, is more likely to buy from you again than someone who has never been your customer. Amazing? Possibly. But true.

## Increase Transaction Frequency

Obviously, if there's a limit to the number of times your product or service can be used by one customer, there's a limit to the number of times they will buy. That, though, is not the only reason for infrequent transactions. A very common one is that they forget about you. If a customer forgets about you, then frankly you should be ashamed of yourself. Don't let it happen. Give the customer enough time to forget about you and some competitor will slip into that gap and take the customer away from you.

So stay in touch with your customers. We've already talked about ways to do that. All the newsletters, mailshots, emails, tweets – these are ways to keep you in people's minds.

A little while ago, I talked to someone who had bought some cheese online. He placed his order through their website and the cheese arrived in the mail. He thought it was lovely cheese and he wanted some more, but he couldn't remember the name of the company he'd bought it from. I was shocked. Not at him – at the company that sold him the cheese. They knew his name, they knew his address, they knew his email address, they knew what he liked – why on earth had they not sent him one or two emails in the two months since he had placed his order? If they weren't emailing him, it's a fair guess that they weren't emailing anybody else. They were allowing their customers to go elsewhere by default. They were assuming that people will always find their way back to them and the reality is that some will, and some won't. "If they want us, they know where we are," is not an expression I ever want to hear from any salesperson. It's YOUR job to stay in touch. Make sure you do it. Please.

While you're sending your emails, tell your customers about any new product you have, and any special offers there may be. For someone like that cheese retailer, I would expect them to be putting together special holiday packages, Eid packages and Christmas packages at appropriate times of the year and letting people know about them.

Something else a company in a business like the cheese shop can consider – *should* consider – is setting up a club that involves a monthly payment. This used to be very popular with record producers when people still bought records instead of downloading music, and it works well today for online wine merchants and people in that sort of business, where there's lots of competition not only online but also in the high street, and the risk of your customer going elsewhere at any time is high, because a lot of these purchases are impulse buys. Someone paying, say, $20 each month (and getting a little something in return, like a regular top up to the account or free delivery or a bonus bottle of wine) is much less likely to go somewhere else. The retailer has locked them in as customers. If there's any way you can do this in your business, do so because it can be extremely effective. A wine merchant in the UK has gone from startup to a large and thriving business in the course of three years. Yes, a detailed knowledge of wine and a web of contacts in wine-growing countries has been a great help, but the two things that have worked best for them are:

- Points awarded for each purchase. A certain number of points gets you a free bottle of wine; *and*
- A referral program whereby any customer who introduces another customer who actually places an order receives £10 towards their next purchase.

Once again, I merely throw this out as an example of what other people are doing. The world is full of innovative, creative marketing ploys like these. Look hard at what other people are doing and see what will work for you. And, as I've already said, don't restrict yourself to looking at what is working in your own industry. It may very well be a completely different marketplace that provides you with your most productive ideas.

# Repeat Buyers Beat One-Time Buyers Hands Down

Hold onto your customers. Don't let them go. If you've been in business for any length of time, you should know by now what the average lifespan of a customer with you is. Extending that lifespan should be a priority objective.

Once again, it won't happen by accident. If you lost customers in the past, spend some time thinking about those account losses and working out why they happened. Be honest with yourself. What lost the account? Was it a personality clash? A product failure? Undercutting by someone else? The emergence of a better product? A failure to stay in touch with the customer often enough? Not responding to a complaint quickly enough? Not dealing as fast as you should have done with a problem?

You may be able to point to a number of those reasons for losing accounts and say, "Yes, that one, that one, and that one – all of those things happened at different times." If you've really been honest with yourself, you will now reap the benefit for that honesty because you can work out strategies for not making those mistakes again. Which means you are working out strategies for not losing accounts again.

And that's the objective.

And since I've asked one awkward question, let me ask another. Do you know your customers as well as you think you do?

The reason I ask that is because, again and again, I've seen consultancy clients describe their relationship with the customer in quite glowing terms, but when I have a chance to examine the actual customer relationship I find that it isn't the way my client thinks it is at all.

There's a natural tendency to which we are all prone (including me) to see things through rose-tinted spectacles. Unless we actually have a serious problem right in front of our eyes, we tend to assume that things are better than, perhaps, they really are.

What I urge you to do is to examine the system you have in place to find out what your customers think of you. And I know, right now, that some people reading this (not necessarily you, but quite a lot of people) will be thinking, "What on earth is she talking about? What does she mean, system? We don't have a system to tell us what people think about us. Or, if we do, the system consists of waiting till somebody complains."

In fact, that is a very common approach – to assume that all is well with the customer relationship unless you actually hear a customer complaint. And it simply won't do. Why not? Because most dissatisfied customers never complain about the problems they are experiencing. They simply find another supplier. Which means that, simply because you didn't have a system in place to tell you what the true state of your customer relationship was, you lose a customer.

You'd like some figures on that? I'll give you some.

Ruby Newell-Legner reports that her research shows that a typical business only hears from 4% of its dissatisfied customers. That leaves 96% who don't say what they are thinking, and 91% never buy from that business again.

That's a shaker, isn't it? Here's another:

An American Express survey showed that 78% of consumers had backed out of a transaction they had already agreed, or not made a purchase they had intended to, because of bad customer service. Had they told the company about the bad customer service? They had not.

One more.

Research by McKinsey says that 70% of buying experiences are based on the way the customer feels they are being treated.

But I asked how you felt you were doing in your relationships with customers. While you're weighing that up, here's a statistic that you may find sobering:

According to researchers Lee Resources:

*80% of companies say they deliver "superior" customer service*
*Only 8% of customers of those same companies agree with them*

I'll say it again. Get serious about finding out how your customers really feel about you. And, if the results aren't good, make putting things right your first priority.

In some sorts of business, management may not know much about the day-to-day dealings with the customers, but there are people in the business who do know. Take, for example, a field maintenance company – one that sends technicians to maintain and fix other businesses' equipment. Those technicians, in fact, are the people best positioned to sell higher value products and to cross sell, but the point I'm making here is that they are also best positioned to know if all is well in the customer relationship or if there is a problem. What is disappointing is that, too often, management has not put in place a mechanism by which the technicians can feed this information back to them and they, after all, are the people who can put the problem right. So examine the way your company is set up, take note of who has most dealings with the customers, and ensure that those people have a route to report on customer problems and are encouraged to do so.

There are some things that are not possible for companies selling large numbers of relatively low value products to a huge number of people, but that work well for businesses with a smaller number of customers who spend rather more money with them. A law firm would be a good example of that. It's a very good idea for businesses in that position to make a point of knowing as much as they can find out (without actually prying) about the customer's background, home life (wife's or husband's name; number of children; what those children are doing; interests outside work – it could become a very long list). You get this information during a casual chat in the office, or at lunch, the squash club, the gym – but the important thing is to write it down as soon as you are out of the customer's sight. Keep it readily available so that you can refresh your memory before a meeting.

And, of course, whatever you do, remember the customer's name. Dale Carnegie said, "A person's name is the sweetest sound." What he meant was that we all like to hear our name spoken. We like to feel that we are recognized. That we are important.

I'd like now to offer some ideas on building your business that I'm going to go through almost at random. Some may feel as though they would work in your business, and some may not, but I hope and believe that there will be something here for everyone.

***Take a good look at your web presence***. Are you blogging? If not, did you know that regular blog posts accompanied by social marketing (at the very least, you should tweet a link to the blog post and put the same link on Facebook) are considered one of the most effective ways of marketing your business? It's not a job for the amateur; whoever writes the blog posts needs to understand SEO and to be up-to-date with the latest changes in algorithms used by search engines, but done properly it can be very effective. An important thing to remember about blog posts is that they work best if they are useful and informative to customers. A blog post is a very soft sell, and the only actual selling it contains may be in the Call To Action (CTA) at the very end.

***An awful lot of money spent on marketing is wasted***. My advice would be, "If you can't measure it, don't do it." Do you actually understand which part of your marketing is working, which part isn't, and why? I imagine everyone's heard about John Wanamaker's remark, "Half the money I spend on advertising is wasted; the trouble is I don't know which half." It's very amusing, but it's also extremely unhelpful. A/B Marketing is one of a number of techniques used to decide what you're doing that provides a reasonable return on investment and what you are doing that doesn't. Get a professional involved, because this is not an area for the amateur. There are some very useful metrics and analytics, but they can be highly technical and need expert interpretation.

*Trade Associations, Service Clubs...* If you are not involved in one of these, you probably should be. Being a member is fine; being on the board is better. Try to join something where you are likely to meet customers and potential customers. Your local Chamber of Commerce may be a very good bet and it may not – check out the membership.

*Giveaways*. I've talked about the need to get referrals and also to get positive reviews. Think about having a contest; for example, everyone who posts a review or refers a new customer during the next month will go into the draw for a shopping voucher.

*Press Releases*. Local newspapers in particular are always desperate for something new to go in their pages, but they don't have much money so their staff are overworked. Find some bit of news about your company – it may be a big new contract you've landed from a country on the other side of the world or it may simply be that the lady who runs the warehouse is taking maternity leave because she's just given birth to a bouncing 8-pound baby boy. Whatever it is, either find out how press releases should be written or get someone who already knows to write it for you, because newspapers are far likelier to use it if it's presented in a way they can lift from the press release directly onto their page.

*Search online* for businesses like yours in distant places. How are they marketing themselves? Do you see anything there that you could adapt to your own needs? Any ideas they have that could also be applicable where you are? Don't be afraid to get inspiration from other people's ideas – it's one of the greatest compliments you can pay them.

*"A satisfied customer is the best business strategy of all."*
Michael LeBoeuf

# Principle 7

# A Customer's Real Value

## What's your return on investment in your customers?

Customers are people, and people are worth more than just money. Nevertheless, for some purposes it's good to work out what a customer is worth in cash terms. That means asking the question, if you can encourage:

- More repeat buying
- Sales of larger average value
- Over a longer period of time

what do you believe might be the total profit from that customer relationship over the time it continues to exist?

It's possible to do the sums. At least, it is if you keep your records in a reasonable state. Let's start with a hypothetical example:

| | |
|---|---|
| Average value of each sale | $1,000 |
| Number of times each year the average customer buys from you | 6.3 |
| Number of years the average customer remains a customer | 3.1 |
| Total number of customers | 1,400 |

Okay; based on those figures the average customer is going to give you revenue of $6,300 for 3.1 years, which is a total over the customer lifetime of $19,530. For the entire customer base, it comes to $27,342,000. That's the total of sales revenue. It is not, of course, the total profit.

Now, in Chapter 6 we outlined four different ways to grow your business. Let's keep things simple and assume that we can get a 5% growth on each of the four heads. This is how the same table will look then:

| | |
|---|---|
| Average value of each sale | $1,050 |
| Number of times each year the average customer buys from you | 6.6 |
| Number of years the average customer remains a customer | 3.3 |
| Total number of customers | 1,470 |

That's not bad, is it? The total lifetime value of a single average customer is now $22,869 and for the entire customer base it has gone to $33,617,430.

The purpose of going through this exercise is to focus attention on the small things, because it's often the small things that are easiest to change. Those four ways of increasing the amount of business you're doing – a 5% increase in each of them should not be particularly hard to achieve, provided that you work on it. And once you've got a 5% increase, you can look to increase it to a 7½% increase. And then a 10% increase. And then…

And each time you bring about that modest increase, the action leads to an increase in sales revenue that is far from modest.

# Income from that customer is $22,869!

Drawing attention to what a customer is worth to the business helps us take a close look at business relationships. Perhaps there's a problem with a particular customer. Perhaps the problem is proving difficult to resolve. Perhaps part of you is tired and feels like saying, "Oh, let it go. So what if we lose one customer? We've got another 1,469."

Yes, okay, you got another 1,469. And if you look at it in those terms, you may feel that losing one customer is no big loss. But now, when you look at that recalcitrant problem, remind yourself that you're not losing one customer; you're losing $22,869 in sales.

Does it feel different now?

Move on from there and remind yourself that every customer who leaves because of dissatisfaction will tell other people. They'll also tell the company they move to and you can bet your life that whoever that competitor is will let people know that your customer was unhappy with you. Because one customer went, you could lose another five and now your total lost sales revenue is $137,214. And that hurts!

### *What About Margin?*

So far, I've talked about total sales revenue. That's important, but it's a little less important than margin – the profit you make on each sale and from each customer. Actually, it's not a little less important; it's a lot less important, because in the long run what keeps you afloat and makes life worth living is the profit you make and not total sales revenue. And even that isn't entirely true, because what really keeps you afloat and makes life worth living is not just the profit you make, but the profit you make that you are able to convert into cash. Investment guru Jim Slater tells his clients to focus on cash. He says that the first place you should turn to when you receive the financial statements of a company in which you hold shares is the Cash Flow Statement.

The reason is that, in the last resort, it is cash that keeps any business – including yours – afloat. What Slater asks is, "If this company is making such wonderful profits, how come it needs to be asking shareholders to stump up for a rights issue? If it's really as profitable as it says it is, it should be returning cash to shareholders, not asking for more." And that is exactly correct.

Discussing how profit turns into cash, and what may sometimes get in the way and prevent that, is beyond the scope of this book. Discuss it with your accountant, because you really do need to understand it. However, examining the difference between sales revenue and profit, and looking at the impact that has on our figures, is relevant and we need to do it. Here is the last table we had, with some lines added:

| Average value of each sale | $1,050 |
|---|---|
| Average gross profit on each sale | $300 |
| Number of times each year the average customer buys from you | 6.6 |
| Number of years the average customer remains a customer | 3.3 |
| Lifetime gross profit per customer | $6,534 |
| Total number of customers | 1,470 |
| Lifetime gross profit for whole customer base | $9,604,980 |

Those figures are a little lower than the ones quoted earlier, but they are more realistic. And if you wonder why I have used gross profit and not net profit, the reason is that this is the figure that has to cover all your operating costs and the fact is that, the more customers you have, the more gross margin there will be to spread those costs over.

I don't know what the figures are in your business – but you do. So you should be able to work out how much it costs you to gain a new customer (Customer Acquisition Cost), what the cost of a lost customer is, and how much it costs to hold onto a customer (Customer Retention Cost). And that may cause you to look differently at some of the decisions I've been talking about in this book.

## Making Rational Spending Decisions

Everyone, when they launch a new business, should draw up a business plan containing financial forecasts. In my experience, the forecasts are usually on the optimistic side, which is how it should be because an entrepreneur needs, above all, to be optimistic about what she or he is getting into. However, once the actual numbers start to become available, it's possible to do the sort of analysis I just walked you through and when you've done that, you will know how much you are able to spend on, for example, winning a new customer or fixing a specific problem that, if left, may cost you five customers. You can make the decision rationally and logically because you have the data you need.

Of course, the amount that you are able to spend and the amount that you are willing to spend may be two different figures and that must remain your decision. What I will say is:

1. If the amount you are willing to spend is less than the amount you are able to spend, I understand your decision
2. If the amount you are willing to spend is more than the amount you are able to spend, I really do recommend caution.

The whole point of having genuine financial data available is to prevent making the sort of decision that can destroy the business. Probably, it is always best to lean towards option 1 of the two I have just listed, because a degree of financial caution is always sensible when running a business.

You can also do some sums to decide how much it is reasonable to spend on business promotion. A business, just like a household, cannot go on spending money it doesn't have. There are two calculations you have to make:

1. Calculate how much the promotion is likely to cost you and how much business it may win for you in the near future
2. Calculate how much additional business the promotion may go on generating into the future

Let's suppose you are thinking of running a seminar for 150 people in a four-star hotel. You'll have a guest speaker who will charge you $1000 plus travel and accommodation costs of $180. Hire of the room itself will be charged at a delegate rate, to include coffee breaks and lunch, of $42, so that – taking into account you, three members of your staff, the guest speaker and the hundred and 50 guests, the total will come to $6,510. Then you plan to give them all dinner after the seminar, for which the hotel quotes a charge of $50 per head for a total of $7,750. You plan that you and two of your staff members who live some distance away will stay the night in the hotel and the discounted room rate for bed and breakfast will be $90 per head.

The whole thing, therefore, is going to cost you $15,710.

Your average gross profit per sale is $300.

Just to break even, you are going to have to make 53 sales that you weren't going to make without the seminar.

So there's the question for you. If you run this seminar for these people with that guest speaker, will it generate at least 53 sales that you would not otherwise have had? If you think the answer is yes, the seminar is a good idea. If you think the answer is no, perhaps you need to look at the idea again.

What I hope I've been able to convey in this chapter is that focusing on individual transactions is not the best way of running your business. Nor is thinking in isolation about almost any of the topics discussed in this book. The fact is that everything works together. Making one sale to one customer doesn't do much for your business. What matters is the lifetime return on investment per customer and the success you have in:

a) Increasing the lifetime return on investment per customer; *and*
b) Increasing the number of customers.

*"You don't learn to walk by following rules. You learn by doing, and by falling over."*

Richard Branson

# What Next?

I promised you seven principles for business success, even in the hardest economies. And I've given you that. This book contains seven principles that a business owner should apply today in order to be successful. Those principles apply even when economic conditions are tough – perhaps especially when economic conditions are tough – but they apply when everything is going well, too. These are seven principles for success, at any time, in any business. And I've given you one chapter for each principle. So why am I going on? What's this additional chapter here for?

It's to convey the message that this is not a one-time thing; that you don't achieve success in business by reading a book, understanding a set of principles, and then getting on with the job. Success is an iterative process and a learning process. You go back again and again – to check the results, to be sure you know what's happening, to adjust the course of the business and, most of all (as Sir Richard Branson's quote above suggests) to learn from your mistakes. Because the well-known saying that the person who never made a mistake never made anything is true.

What should you do now? You should make a plan, based on this book, showing how you propose to put into effect the things you have learned.

## 1. MAKE IT HAPPEN

"The longest journey begins with a single step." Start by looking at how the seven principles can be applied to your business. Every business is different (even when they are in the same industry) and nothing should be applied without thought. If one way to apply one of these principles doesn't work, find another way to put it into practice.

It's your business. You know the history, the people involved, the context, the products. Adapt what you've read to work with the reality you face.

## 2. PRIORITISE TARGETS THROUGH RESEARCH

Go back to the beginning of the book. Read what I said about setting targets. Accept that you can't change every single thing at once and you have to set priorities for each of those targets. The priorities will be based on what is most important, but also on what is possible. There may be things you want to do and intend to do that you can't yet do because you can't afford them or because some other change has to be in place first. Don't lose sight of those, but don't get hung up on them, either. You will get there.

Don't spurn opportunities. Remember what William Arthur Ward said: "Opportunities are like sunrises. If you wait too long, you miss them." Remember, too, that the world is full of opportunities. The trick isn't being lucky, or being in the right place at the right time; the trick is seeing an opportunity. It's amazing how many people don't. Research isn't the only way to find opportunity, but it's one of them and it's a good one.

## 3. TAKE IT PERSONALLY

The process you are embarking on is one of change. When you're making far-reaching changes, it's a good idea to keep checking how things are going. Are you still on target? Have the changes you are making uncovered problems that you didn't anticipate? (You'll be an unusual business if the answer to that question is "No"). Don't go into any of this with a rigid attitude that, "It has to be this way." At each stage of the journey, consider the options. Decide which will work best for you.

And that means think about how things affect *you*, and what *you* can take from them.

## 4. IMPLEMENT. THEN IMPLEMENT. THEN IMPLEMENT AGAIN. NEVER GIVE UP

Look at the Richard Branson quotation again. Business is complicated. You're making internal changes in an environment that is probably also subject to external change. Of course there are going to be setbacks, but following these seven principles, you are on the right road. Keep going. You will like it when you get there.

While you go about putting into practice what you've read in this book, you'll see chances to make a difference – to other people's lives; to your own life; to your business. Chance is wonderful – IF it's taken. Seize it. Put it into practice. Become known as a doer. Because the successes in this world are the doers.

## 5. MONITOR

In Chapter 7, I talked about figures: establishing what they are, working with them, monitoring them. Never stop that. When the British General Electric Company had seven divisions and more than a hundred companies, the Chief Exec received on his desk every morning the overnight figures for each of those companies. Any untoward deviations from plan and he was on the phone to the managing director of that company. British GEC was perhaps the most successful conglomerate in the UK at that time.

You probably don't have anything like that number of reports to look at, but you need your finger on the pulse – you need to know what is happening, and that doesn't just mean talking to people; it means watching the numbers.

## THE END OF THE BOOK IS ALSO THE BEGINNING

It's the end of the book – but it's also the beginning of a whole new phase in your life. A phase of success, profitability and the satisfaction of knowing you're now equipped for one of the most exciting enterprises there are. You have the tools you need. Now,

### *GO FOR IT!*

Join Carrie Anne Yu global networking community and connect with like-minded people around the world! https://www.facebook.com/carrieanneyuspeak/

If this book has whetted your appetite to work with Carrie Anne Yu, leave a message on www.globalwise.media or email me at carrie@globalwise.media and I'll be back to you within 48 hours, max.

# About the Author

Carrie Anne Yu is an author, speaker and business consultant. She is the CEO & Founder of Globalwise Media, a business consultation and digital marketing agency. Her business focuses on helping business owners, consultants, coaches and professional service specialists to grow their customer base, increase revenue and maximize profit.

Carrie is dedicated to helping professionals grow their businesses through her writing, speaking and consulting. She has internationally published two business books "Create Lifetime Loyal Customers – 7 Success Principles To Attract More Customers In ANY Business Even In The Toughest Economies" and "The Ultimate List Building Training Guide – Build a Qualified Customer Base With The Ultimate Techniques" in the year 2016.

Printed in the United States
By Bookmasters